THE BIRTH OF HEROIN

AND

THE DEMONIZATION

OF

THE DOPE FIEND

THE BIRTH OF HEROIN
AND
THE DEMONIZATION
OF
THE DOPE FIEND

by Th. Metzger

Loompanics Unlimited
Port Townsend, Washington

The Birth of Heroin and The Demonization of The Dope Fiend
© 1998 by Th. Metzger

Published by:
Loompanics Unlimited
PO Box 1197
Port Townsend, WA 98368
Loompanics Unlimited is a division of Loompanics Enterprises, Inc.
1-360-385-2230
E-mail:loompanx@olympus.net
Web site: www.loompanics.com

Cover illustration by Nick Bougas

ISBN 1-55950-177-4
Library of Congress Card Catalog 98-65205

Contents

Chapter One
God's Own Medicine

1.

God's Own Medicine came to America on the May-flower, landing with the Pilgrims in 1620.[1] Opium dissolved in wine and scented with saffron, cinnamon and cloves was called laudanum. Opium in tincture form (mixed with licorice, honey, benzoic acid, camphor and anise oil) was known as paregoric. Both of these opiate elixirs were carried ashore soon after the Puritans established their foothold in the New World. And in the almost 400 years that followed, opiates have been a constant presence in American culture: a much-heralded medical necessity and tainted play-toy, profoundly American and at the same time a baleful "foreign influence" corrupting the body politic, both demon seed and God's Own Medicine.

The Puritan colonists fled Europe to keep themselves and their children pure; taint-terrors are always about the offspring, the sanctity of the seed. They traveled to the New World to begin again the great work of their God. As courageous as they were ill-tempered, God-and-Satan-haunted, hard-shell, hard-buckle Calvinist warriors, they waded ashore on the ice-crusted "dessart" beach of New England, and with them came an Old World (in fact, Neolithic) presence: the fruit of the opium poppy.

It was winter, "sharp and violent... cruel and fierce." The land they came to was a "hideous and desolate wilderness, full of wild beasts and wild men." Behind them lay 1,000 leagues of pitiless sea. Before them lay "a whole country... wild and savage." In their first winter — called

The Starving Time — half their number died; diseased, frozen, hungry.[2]

However, the colony did survive until spring, and when the Mayflower returned to England, only the mariners, not a single Puritan, went back with it.

Among those who survived was a doctor: Samuel Fuller by name. A widower, aged 30 years, a deacon of the church, Dr. Fuller brought with him — along with his surgical fleam for bleeding patients, his clyster syringe, his forceps and bonesaw — a brass and rosewood medicine chest. Roughly cubical when closed up, the chest had a slot for the skeleton key and a brass carrying handle. The top opened, freeing two side portions or wings to swing out. Two drawers slid out from underneath. The chest held 16 vials of medicine. Of coarse green glass, with wide, flanged mouths, these vials held a variety of medical nostrums. Beside emetics for inducing "a smart vomit," Spanish fly caustic (useful for making counterirritant blisters), and chinchona bark extractives, Dr. Fuller had brought to the New World paregoric and laudanum. Other than alcohol, opium was at this time the only item in the *materia medica* which truly had the power to subdue pain.[3]

It took weeks for the Puritans to decide on a place to establish their colony. Scouting parties in a shallop coasted about Cape Cod, spray freezing to their coats in shiny glazes, shadowy Indian forms gliding in and out of sight. When the spot was finally chosen, the belongings of the colonists were ferried in from the Mayflower. At what point the medicine chest — with the vials of opium packed neatly in pine shavings and woolen lint — was brought in is not recorded. But it did land, carried like the Israelite's Ark of the Covenant. Two men waded through the frozen salt surf, up the broken stone shingle, and like the Spaniards who'd placed a flag to claim the new conquest for their sovereign, set the medicine chest down and claimed this spot as theirs. A Bible, of course, preceded the opium, firearms, food and homey furnishings, too, but the opium elixirs did land, and took their place, to rest like a cornerstone on the harsh, barren, New England soil.

Though the common image of the Puritans is that of haters of pleasure, bitter opponents of all physical comfort, in fact they brought along with them much alcohol: "strong waters" (gin), aqua vitae (brandy), and beer. Indeed, their thirst for beer — according to their first historian, William Bradford — was a matter of considerable significance early on in the colony's life.[4] Though drunkenness was frowned on, beer was staple in many Puritan homes, fortifying the men in their dawn-to-dusk battles against the wilderness, killing the pain and giving them a taste of the homeland they'd fled forever.

Laudanum and paregoric did not come to the New World as agents of idle pleasure, however. They were brought along to alleviate physical suffering. The complex interplay of pain and pleasure is one of the deepest currents in the story of opiates in the U.S. Americans are deeply conflicted about pain and pleasure; both are valued, and at the same time neither is embraced wholeheartedly. Certainly the Puritans made the notions of reward and suffering a significant element in their worldview. One hundred and two warriors of purity, minions of a fierce and relentless deity, the Puritans ground their moral axes to a silvery sheen on the rough stone of New England's coast. They saw their travails in apocalyptic terms:

> When god is about to turn the earth into Paradise, he does not begin his work where there is some good growth already, but in a wilderness, where nothing grows, and nothing is to be seen but dry sand and barren rock, that the light may shine out of the darkness.[5]

And it was indeed a war of light against darkness that the Puritans set out to win. The climate, the land itself, the flora, were all perceived in demonic terms. The native inhabitants were doubly so: the archetypal dark-skinned Others who would be eradicated by muskets and torches if God didn't rout them out first with pestilence.

If the Puritan sojourn in the New World was part of God's plan, then the Indians were not bit players but important antagonists. Early in their invasion of the Americas, Europeans conceived of the native inhabitants as symbols, mythic figures. They were paradoxically both base flesh and enemies in a cosmic spiritual war. On one hand, Cotton Mather described them as "rattle-snakes" and "barbarians." On the other, they were "people of the Devil," and "infidels." Their lord and master was unquestionably Satan, who Mather calls in *Wonders of the Invisible World* a "small black man."

One of the first captivity narratives ever published is that of Mary Rowlandson. In it, she describes her Indian captors as "atheistical, proud, wild, cruel, barbarous, brutish, (in one word) diabolical."[6] Robert Berkhofer has done an excellent job of tracing the evolution of the European concept of "Indian." One of his most important points is that the white man reconceived the 2,000+ ethnic groups in the New World as a monolithic culture, sharing a set of sinister characteristics:

Nakedness and lechery, passion and vanity led to lives of polygamy and sexual promiscuity among themselves and constant warfare and fiendish revenge against their enemies. When habits and customs were not brutal they appeared loathsome to Whites. Cannibalism and human sacrifice were the worst sins, but cruelty to captives and incessant warfare ranked not far behind in the estimation of Whites. Filthy surroundings... indolence rather than industry, improvidence in the face of scarcity, thievery and treachery... superstition represented by the "conjurers" and "medicine men," the hard slavery of women and laziness of men.[7]

This list might as easily describe the early 20th century Dope Fiend as it does the 17th century "Indian." The heathen — whether native American, Chinese, Black, or more nebulously alien — continues to haunt the American soul. The dark dopple-ganger, tainted by ill-defined sin, only quasi-human, would emerge again and again to plague and torment pure, white America. Usually this malign specter was in league with some devil, or was the devil himself. It's crucial, in order to understand the development of the Dope Fiend, to start at the beginning. The Puritan's world-view echoes to the present day. And their concept of the demonic, dark-skinned Other (the "small black man" with his legion of hell-born followers) has appeared again and again, usually in times of cultural chaos or external threat. The Dope Fiend is as much a mythic figure as an actual social phenomenon. His roots reach back to the very first day opium landed in the New World.

2.

Though the Puritans died out as a cohesive denomination, they nonetheless lived on. Their descendants, their morality, their obsessional combative world-view spread westward across the continent. The land was conquered, the Indian "savages" were subdued (or uneasily subsumed) and a new civilization flourished.

A hundred years after the Puritans had effectively vanished from North America, opium, "the pure white pearl of healing," was embedded deep in New World culture. During the heydays of American opiate use — the middle- to late-1800s — doctors referred to the drug as God's Own Medicine. "The great and immortal" physician William Osler was still using the term as late as 1894.[8] Whether they were aware of opium's centuries-long association with divine powers of healing is not clear, but whatever the reason — bravado, historical continuity, ironic blasphemy — the 19th century medical man's term echoed the long-standing belief that God himself had given opium to humankind as a gift.

The dried tears of the unripe *papaver somniferum* had been eaten raw and smoked for millennia. The plant, though often associated with China, is thought to be a native to the mountains of southern Asia. It is the great innovator Paracelsus who is generally credited with introducing opium into Western medicine. Like an evangelist, Paracelsus traveled throughout Europe with the drug in the pommel of his saddle. Calling it the "stone of immortality," he owed much of his success to the enthusiastic — some would say Messianic — way in which he dispensed the drug.

His followers were equally taken with its healing powers, and soon many serious medical practitioners were praising it as a therapeutic paragon, the greatest conqueror of pain that God had ever provided. Paracelsus probably coined the term laudanum. To create the pill form, he mixed up one quarter-weight of opium, hensbane juice, mummia (the dried flesh of mummified human bodies), salts of pearls and corals, bone of the heart of the stag, bezoar stone (an intestinal concretion found in goats and gazelles), amber, musk and "unicorn." His liquid laudanum contained the juice of oranges and lemons, cloves, ambergris and saffron, all mixed into a wine-tincture of opium.[9]

Thomas Sydenham, the founding father of clinical medicine, the so-called English Hippocrates, stated his belief in opium's divine nature in no uncertain terms: "Among the remedies which has pleased almighty God to give to man to relieve his sufferings, none is so universal and so efficacious as opium."[10] Dr. Benjamin Rush, after whose "heroic therapy" heroin was named, also was a confirmed believer in opium's value. In the treatment of cholera, he claimed, "recourse must be had to opiates. A few drops of liquid laudanum combined in a testaceous julip, with peppermint or cinnamon-water, would soothe the stomach and bowels." For the relief of intestinal spasms, Rush instructed physicians to use enemas "made of flaxseed tea, or of mutton broth, or of starch dissolved in water, with a few drops of liquid laudanum in them."[11] Jonathan Pereira's well-regarded textbook of therapeutics updated Rush's assertions, proclaiming that opium was "undoubtedly the most important and valuable remedy in the whole *materia medica*."[12] Dr. George Wood's praise for opium was — if possible — even more fervent:

There is not the same uncontrollable excitement as from alcohol, but an exhaltation of our better mental qualities, a warmer glow of benevolence, a higher devotional spirit, and with a stronger self-reliance, and consciousness of power... For the intellectual and imaginative faculties are raised to the point compatible with individual capacity. The poet has never had brighter fancies, or deeper feelings, or greater felicity of expression, nor the philosopher a more penetrating or profounder insight than when under the influence of opium in this stage of its actions. It seems to make the individual, for the time, a better and greater man.[13]

Eleven years later, the president of the American Gynecological Society, Dr. T. Gaillard Thomas, declared that "for the relief of pain, the treatment is all summed up in one word, and that is *opium*. This divine drug overshadows all other anodynes... There is a natural tendency in the human race to take opium."[14] Oliver Wendell Holmes Sr., no friend to religious fanatics (in fact a vocal critic of Puritan excesses), also saw opium as a gift from God. It was, according to this dean of the Harvard Medical School, a substance "...which the creator himself seems to prescribe, for we often see the scarlet poppy growing in the corn fields, as if it were foreseen that wherever there is hunger to be fed, there must be pain to be soothed."[15]

Opium reached the American population in a wide variety of forms. The Black Drop, a celebrated curative of the early 1800s, had three times the pain-killing power of laudanum. Containing no alcohol, the Black Drop was a concoction of opium dissolved in the juice of crab apples, and flavored with nutmeg, saffron, yeast and sugar. The result — pitchy, viscous, vilely sweet — was used by thousands to relieve the suffering of uncountable ailments. Dover's Powder, another much beloved preparation, was a standard item in most American apothecaries: an admixture of opium and ipecac (pulverized Brazil root).

Between 1800 and 1900, the amount of opium consumed by Americans rose steadily. Exact numbers are impossible to come by; the amount of smuggled and domestically produced opium will never be known. But legal imports increased as the century wore on. For example, between 1860 and 1869, 110,305 pounds of opium were imported into the U.S. by legal means. By the last decade of the century, this number had risen to half a million pounds.[16] Barrels, crates, and hogsheads of opium were unloaded from seafaring vessels at America's major ports. Entirely legal at this time, it was processed in pharmaceutical labs and sent by rail into the heartland.

Victorian opiate consumption was enormous compared to today's. Yet the picture of the shaking, filthy, rapacious skeletal slave to opium is almost never seen until the early 1900s. The not-so-distant descendant of the savage Indian, the heathen Chinese, and the "brute Negro," the so-called Dope Fiend was a creation of the late Victorian mind. Even the term "addict" only took on its current meaning well after the Golden Age of Opiates. An addict in the 1800s was a person deeply involved with, or fascinated by, any number of subjects. Books, wine, the company of "immoral women," wit, racing, coffee, dice and sea: all of these were literal addictions in the 1800s. The late 20th century notion of addiction would be very foreign to an American opiate user living 100 years before. The transformation of the opiate user comprises much of the later portion of this book. But it's important to note early on that tens of thousands of Americans used opium preparations — many on a daily basis — and the climate of opinion did not condemn these men and women as pariahs, carriers of moral contagion, or threats to societal order. What occurred between 1880 and 1930 was not merely a redefinition of the term "addict," but a radical shift in understanding. The fiend, the spawn of darkness, had emerged again from his occult (magical and hidden) lair.

3.

Opiates flowed to the general population in two broad streams: through self-diagnosis and medication, and as prescribed by doctors.

Morphine, heroin's direct ancestor, was isolated by F.W. Serturner in 1803. Opium's principal ingredient, morphine was the form in which the 19th century doctor most often used the drug. It is in effect the essence of opium, and was named by its discoverer after Morpheus, the Greek god of sleep.

The American Civil War did more to create the desire and need for morphine than any other force. More soldiers died in the conflict from diarrheic dysentery than from gunshot wounds. And morphine provided relief for both these conditions, "binding the bowels" and killing the pain of torn and infected tissue. By hypodermic injection and in pill form, the drug was dispensed in huge quantities. One Union doctor was well known for pouring morphine into the palm of his hand, "in carefully portioned doses," and having sick soldiers line up to lick their medicine like dogs. Such was the impact of the Civil War that afterward the heavy use of morphine was known as the "soldier's disease."

Post-war morphine use was no self-indulgent whim. "Maimed and shattered survivors from a hundred battlefields, diseased and disabled soldiers released from hostile prisons, anguished and hopeless wives and mothers made so by the slaughter of those dearest to them, have found, many of them, temporary relief from their suffering in opium," wrote Dr. Horatio Day in his 1868 book *The Opium Habit.*[17]

Roughly one in 25 Americans were heavy users in the late 1800s, a number far greater than today's. Doctors wrote prescriptions which could be filled at any local pharmacy, the kindly, avuncular druggist mixing up gallons of tinctured opium for wives and husbands, young and old. Physicians also sold directly to their patients, and countless times brought out the hypodermic needle for a quick and surefire cure for any number of complaints. Dr. H.H. Kane's 1880 textbook *The Hypodermic Injection of Morphia* lists over 50 diseases for which morphine could be useful, everything from tuberculosis, pneumonia and diabetes to nymphomania, vaginusmus, prenatal nausea and insanity. Fifteen years later, Dr. Samuel Potter claimed in his well regarded pharmaceutical textbook, "probably no drug in the *materia medica* is so useful as opium, or has so wide a range of applications."[18]

Combine the brutality of the Civil War with the grinding, unrelenting misery of life in the new "gilded age" factories and urban hovels, and the result is a condition for which many believed opiates were the only cure. And considering the fact that respiratory diseases were the leading cause of death in the 19th century (hundreds of thousands of Americans breathing their viruses and bacterial effluvia on each other in sweatshops, hacking their lungs out in lightless warrens), it should come as no surprise that opiates were so widely used. In the absence of antibiotics, and with only a rudimentary notion of antisepsis, morphine preparations were a godsend: calming agonizing coughs, tranquilizing, killing both physical and emotional pain, and, for some, providing fleeting doses of pleasure.

The Birth of Heroin and
The Demonization of The Dope Fiend

Though not an American invention, patent medicines reached their apotheosis in the United States. The American genius — invention and promotion in equal doses — found a perfect vehicle in proprietary medicines. Purchased by mail, from traveling sales extravaganzas (with comedy, song, juggling, and magic as preamble to the pitch), and off grocery and general store shelves, these concoctions were the mainstay of healing for sufferers who lacked either access to medical care or had little trust in it. Before the Federal Pure Food and Drug Act of 1906, hundreds of patent medicines were available, many of them laced with opium, most of them alcohol-based: pain killers, cough elixirs, anodynes, specifics, women's friends, mother's helpers, soothing syrups, electuaries, opodelocs, cordials, bitters, carminatives and catholicons.

The bewildering array of claims, the bizarre names, and the sheer variety and number of patent medicines available were testimony to the greed of the merchants and the need of the buying public.

An illustration from *Collier's* magazine drawing attention
to the sinister array of patent medicines.

Some patent medicines were targeted at specific conditions:

- Dr. Goodman's American Anti-Gonorrhea Pills
- Aromatic Lozenges of Steel (for sexual debility)
- Pink Pills for Pale People

Some attempted to beguile the buyer with references to supernatural or spectacular forces:

- Lightning Oil
- Dr. Hamlin's Wizard Oil
- Resurrection Pills
- Ambrosial Oil
- Paradise Oil

Some made claims to scientific innovation:

- Dr. Judge's Oxy-Hydrogenated Air
- Radam's Microbe Killer
- Boothman's Pure Phlogiston Cure-All

(D) 1887

Even that paragon of American invention — Thomas A. Edison — produced and sold his own narcotic remedy with the pseudo-scientific name "Poly-Form." This "boon to the sufferer" was compounded of morphine, chloroform, ether, chloral hydrate, alcohol and spices.

Thomas Alva Edison later exploited Chinese stereotypes in his films.
(Courtesy of Dictionary of American Portraits)

Some patent-medicine mongers attempted to excite the buyer's interest by association with foreign lands:
- Bragg's Arctic Liniment
- Wyncoop's Iceland Pectoral
- Hoofland's Greek Oil

- Japanese Life Pills
- Roman Eye Balsam
- Jayne's Spanish Alternative
- Osgood's Indian Cholagogue

Some are simply inexplicable:

- Dr. Tichenor's Antiseptic Refrigerant
- Comstock's Dead-shot Pellets
- Golden Liquid Beef Tonic

And a number were aimed directly at curing so-called female troubles:

- Bradfield's Female Regulator
- Lydia Pinkham's Vegetable Compound (21% alcohol, though the highly successful Miss Pinkham was a vocal supporter of temperance).

Quite a few — with names such as Grandma's Tyke-Relaxant and Baby-Ease — were sold to mothers who would try anything to calm and quiet their children. Often these remedies contained opiates. Mrs. Winslow's Soothing Syrup, for instance, had on average .05 grams of morphine in every bottle.

Thousands of Americans became heavy users of these preparations without any knowledge of their opiate content. But for those who wished to end their dependence on morphine, a number of patent medicines were available. Unfortunately, they invariably contained the drug which they claimed to be freeing the sufferer from. Pronto, Opacura, DeNarco, and Pierce's Golden Discovery were laced with opium. Likewise, drinking cures were heavily touted, most containing alcohol. The percentage varied widely, but amounts as high as 44% alcohol (in Hostetter's Bitters) were not uncommon.

It's a mistake to assume that Americans were merely dim-witted or self-deluded. Their doctors were as much to blame as they were. By 1899, nine out ten physicians were prescribing proprietary medicines. Surveying his mail for that year, a professor at Yale Medical School found that barely half of the 424 medical circulars he'd received were not for questionable quack preparations.[19]

Even that behemoth of American commerce — Sears and Roebuck — was involved in America's love affair with opium. In 1900, their catalog offered two ounces of laudanum ("directions on each bottle for young and old") for 18¢, or one and a half pints for two dollars. Their paregoric ("always useful for children and adults") was available by mail order for 12¢.[20]

And what was the outcome of this massive opium binge? Did the nation witness crazed "addicts" on a rampage of murder and robbery? The collapse of Victorian social order? White slavery? Racial revolt? There was indeed crime, poverty and abuses aplenty in the last decade of the 19th century, but they had very little to do with opiate use.

The average habitué (the most common term in this period) was white, from 30 to 40 years old, female and of the middle or upper class. And there were as many living in the rural South as in the "teeming and blighted" slums of northern cities. Some prostitutes did use opium to numb the sufferings caused by their profession. But generally the opium-user in the Victorian period was a profoundly ordinary woman. She may have been bored, hemmed in by oppressive social roles, visited by illnesses for which there were no cures, but hardly the vicious, contagiously degraded Dope Fiend that popular culture became so enamored with later on.

The medical profession was well aware of this situation. For instance, turn-of-the-century medical textbooks by James Anders and James French both note that heavy morphine use was more common among women than men.[21] Alonzo Calkins describes the typical morphinist as "the lady of the haut-ton, idly lolling upon her velvety fauteuil and vainly trying to cheat the lagging hours that intervene ere the 'clockwork tintinabulum' shall sound the hour for opera or whist."[22]

Women without careers, women of the upper classes who had only to produce an occasional baby to keep the family line intact, women who were little more than ornaments, living/breathing symbols of domestic normalcy: these were the Americans who most often found themselves dependent on opiates.

Catherine Ransome of Rolla, Missouri, can stand as a representative for thousands of her sisters. She was brought up to be a good wife: orderly, religious (though not exceedingly so), attractive, bright but not too bright, selfless. And these qualities were quite enough to catch a husband, a man no less decent than herself. A picture-frame merchant 15 years her senior, Charles Ransome was successful enough in business that they had servants for all their daily household tasks. So Mrs. Ransome was relegated to the position of domestic *genius loci*. Once she'd given birth to their four children, Mrs. Ransome's only real function was to stand as a cornerstone of normalcy. All the other elements of their home life were built on the fundamental innocuousness of her life: needlepoint, a few desultory Chopin études on the piano-forte, tepid conversation. In brief, Catherine Ransome was not so much useless as easily replaceable. With her crushing boredom and ill-defined self-loathing came a return of childhood migraines. And to counter these, her doctor prescribed morphine-laced patent medicines which did reduce — or take the edge off — the vague misery of her life. She spent the rest of her days as a heavy opiate user. Morning, noon and night she took a tablespoon of Mrs. Lambert's Ladies Elixer: 23% alcohol with 40 milligrams of morphine in every squat, square, honey-brown bottle.[23]

A woman who chose to remain nameless wrote of her attachment to morphine in terms that might seem odd to modern readers:

> I am the last woman in the world to make excuses for my acts, but you don't know what morphine means to some of us, many of us, modern women without professions, without beliefs. Morphine makes life possible. It adds to truth a dream. What more does religion do? Perhaps I shock you. What I mean is that truth alone is both not enough and too much for us. Each of us must add to it his or her dream, believe me. I have added mine; I am really morphine mad, I suppose, but I have enough will left not to go beyond my daily allowance.[24]

Religion, beliefs, dreams, truth: these are not usually the concepts we associate with heavy morphine use. But clearly in this woman's case the use of the drug is as much about meaning and identity as it is about crude physical need.

Before 1870, most doctors viewed the overuse of opiates as a vice, "indulged in by weak-willed and sinful but otherwise normal persons."[25] Dependence, though widespread and often caused by the doctors themselves, was considered unvirtuous, not evidence of pathology. The responsibility of the medical men was fiercely debated: was it indeed their duty to control the wickedness or weakness of their patients? Dr. Oliver, in 1871, defined the profession clearly as an ethical watchdog, claiming that all physicians should be "...responsible for the moral as well as physical welfare of their patients."[26] H.H. Kane also wrote of the opiate users "contracting this habit" at the hands of guilty doctors.[27] Most physicians were well aware at this time that the majority of users were of the middle and upper classes. A census of opiate use in 1878 for instance, stated that "the influence of vicious association was relatively negligible" and that "underworld influences such as prostitution, gambling, etc. largely can be eliminated."[28] In other words, doctors understood that they were at fault. Drs. Jouet, Hull, and Paton wrote about the "vice" being primarily an affliction of the moneyed classes.[29]

Thousands of anonymous women were life-long opium habitués. But also some of the most prominent men of this period went to the needle on a daily basis. Edward Levinstein stated in his 1877 work, *The Morbid Craving for Morphia*, that he was familiar with many opiate users in "the foremost rank of science and art."[30] A prime example is William Stewart Halsted (1852-1922).

Proud scion of a well-heeled, well-regarded New York family, captain of the Yale football team, a founder of the John's Hopkins Medical School, and an innovator in surgical techniques, Dr. Halsted also lived the last 30 years of his life as a daily user of morphine. Closed up in his private chambers, he'd take off his jacket, roll up his shirt sleeve, twist a rubber tourniquet around his upper arm and slide in the hypodermic needle. Like hundreds of other doctors who used morphine, Halsted's supply was pure and nearly limitless. He also had state-of-the-art equipment which no one would think odd to be in his possession. Switching from medical-grade cocaine at the age of 34, Halsted gave himself a maintenance dose of 180 mg. of morphine a day, though he later scaled back to 90 mg.[31]

Besides an illustrious career in medicine, Halsted married into a distinguished Southern family and had by all accounts a happy and harmonious marriage. At the time of his death, at age 70, still at the top of his profession, only two or three people were aware that he'd been a constant user of morphine for over half his life.

Halsted's medical contributions lie in three areas: the perfection of local anesthesia, the concept of operating-room asepsis, and as the "father of modern surgery." In 1884, after a series of experiments on himself, Halsted was the first surgeon to accomplish true local anesthesia, numbing an entire limb by the precise injection of cocaine into the nerve supplying it. Building on Lister's notion of antisepsis, Halsted developed asepsis: keeping the operating room, the opening into the patient's body, the instruments, and the doctors and nurses themselves as free from bacteria as possible. Just as significant was his technique with the scalpel and probe. Precision and delicacy were his trademarks. Instead of the traditional chop and slash method of surgery (the intensity of the pain requiring lightning-fast cutting), Halsted used deft, light, sparing motions with the surgical blades, keeping tissue damage and bleeding to a minimum. Without these contributions, the progress of surgery would be perhaps decades behind where it is today. In short, William Halsted was both one of America's most important medical pioneers and also a life-long "drug addict."

Among professionals who were heavy users, doctors were the most common, compelled to work long hours in often unbearable conditions, able to prescribe and dispense to themselves. But other life-long morphinists came from the ranks of politics, science, education and even the clergy. The drug was freely available, manufactured by reputable companies (many of them now leaders in the pharmaceutical field), sold in pure form so that standard dosing could be maintained. And though there was a stigma attached to the opiate habit, it was perceived more as an embarrassment than a threat to social order. That these men were so-called Brain Workers — supposedly of a more refined "nervous constitution" — made morphine use more acceptable for them than for the lower orders. "Beside pain and disease, there is a nervous strain of Modern Life, or the 'Mania Americana' which is temporarily relieved by the soothing effects of opium."[32] Harvey Wiley, in 1912, summed up the situation this way: the use of opiates was not generally considered "un-American" but "peculiarly American."[33]

Notes:

1. Trebach, Arnold. *The Heroin Solution.* (Yale U.P.) 1982. p. 38.
2. Bradford, William. *Of Plymouth Plantation.* (NY: Knopf) 1976. p. 62.
3. Ames, Azel. *The Mayflower and Her Log.* (Boston: Houghton Mifflin) 1901. p. 175.
4. Bradford, William. *Of Plymouth Plantation.* (NY: Knopf) 1976. p. 65.

5. Edwards, Jonathan. "Paradise in America." in: *Puritanism and the American Experience.* Editor: Michael McGiffert. (Reading, MA: Addison Wesley) 1969. p. 162.
6. Rowlandson, Mary. *The Sovereignty and Goodness of God.* (Cambridge, MA: Samuel Green) 1682. p. iv.
7. Berknofer, Robert. *The White Man's Indian.* (NY: Knopf) 1978. p. 28.
8. Terry, Charles and Mildred Pellens. *The Opium Problem.* (NY: Committee on Drug Addictions) 1928. p. 104.
9. Wooten, A.C. *Chronicles of Pharmacy Vol. II.* (London: MacMillan) 1910. p. 142.
10. Trebach, Arnold. *The Heroin Solution.* (Yale U.P.) 1982. p. 38.
11. Rush, Benjamin. "An Inquiry Into the Case of the Cholera." in: *Medical Inquiries and Observations. Vol. 1.* (Philadelphia: Pritchard and Hall) 1789. p. 112.
12. Pereira, Jonathan. *The Elements of the Materia Medica.* (Philadelphia) 1854. p. 1039.
13. Wood, George B. *A Treatise on Therapeutics and Pharmacology or Materia Medica.* (Philadelphia: Lippincott). 1868. p. 712.
14. Thomas, T. Gaillard. "Clinical Lecture on the Diseases of Women." *Medical Record.* (16) 1879. p. 316.
15. Holmes, Oliver W. Sr. *Medical Essays 1842-1882.* (Boston: Houghton Mifflin). 1883. p. 202.
16. Lindesmith, Alfred. *Addiction and Opiates.* (Chicago: Aldine) 1968. p. 212.
17. Terry, Charles and Mildred Pellens. *The Opium Problem.* (NY: Committee on Drug Addictions) 1928. p. 5.

18. Potter, n.p.
19. Young, James. *Toadstool Millionaires.* (Princeton U.P.) 1961. p. 160.
20. *Sears Roebuck and Co. Catalog 1900.* Editor: Joseph Schroeder. (Chicago: Follett) 1970. p. 26.
21. Anders and French, *A Textbook Of The Practice Of Medicine.* (Philadelphia, W.B. Saunders) 1899.
22. Calkins, Alonzo. *Opium and the Opium Appetite.* (Philadelphia: Lippincott) 1871. p. 163.
23. Van Ness, Robert. *Catherine Ransome: a Life.* (New York: Henry Holt) 1926. p. 137-138.
24. Courtwright, David. *Dark Paradise.* (Harvard U.P.) 1982. p. 60.
25. *Ibid.,* p. 126.
26. Terry, Charles and Mildred Pellens. *The Opium Problem.* (NY: Committee on Drug Addictions) 1928. p. 94.
27. *Ibid.,* p. 97.
28. *Ibid.,* p. 11.
29. *Ibid.,* pp. 98, 99, and 107.
30. *Ibid.,* p. 138.
31. Coon, George. *William Stewart Halsted: A Life.* (New York, Feinmann Co.) 1943. p. 127.
32. Terry, Charles and Mildred Pellens. *The Opium Problem.* (NY: Committee on Drug Addictions) 1928. p. 113.
33. Wiley, Harvey. "An Opium Bonfire." *Good Housekeeping.* August 1912. p. 252.

Chapter Two
The Devil's Laboratory

1.

Black becomes white; foul useless dregs are transformed into a priceless commodity. The word "alchemy" is too often bandied about in discussions of the chemical industry's headlong advances, but perhaps here — in the case of heroin's birth — it's apt.

Heroin stands as the preeminent "white drug," a curious term when its associations with non-white peoples is considered. The original heroin was the essence of chemical purity, unlike its grandparent, opium, or the later street-quality versions. The essence of contamination, heroin was paradoxically a hyper-refined substance. And it's fitting that heroin was developed, tested, manufactured and marketed by the company that did so much to establish the primacy of "real, genuine, pure" pharmaceuticals: Bayer of Elberfeld, Germany.

Bayer — enriched by pristine white heroin and innocuous tablets of aspirin — was built on the black, stinking ooze left over from one of the filthiest of all industrial processes. This residue from coal gas extraction formed the foundation of not just Bayer however, but the entirety of modern chemical industry: plastics, fertilizers, explosives, synthetic fibers and rubber, drugs, etc.

For decades, chemists considered coal tars a useless by-product. Countless freight cars delivered their loads to gas plants in Europe and America. There, the coal was heated to 1000° C in a vacuum, liberating valuable illuminating gas. It wasn't until 1856 that British chemists discovered coal tar's great worth: the rainbow of dyes locked in the foul, slimy residue. Like the chaotic heaps of organic matter which Dr. Frankenstein sifted through to build his creature, so too the mountains of coal tar could be separated into component parts — classified and stored — and recombined to create hundreds of valuable new items.

In steel-lined vats holding up to a million gallons, the coal tars collected. After the watery portion rose to the surface, the tars were drawn off the bottom. Technicians then used a variety of processes to purify the components: cooling, passing superheated steam through, gravitational separation, washing with caustic soda and sulphuric acid, centrifuging and hot pressing. By the time heroin was born — in 1898 — over 200 substances had been isolated from coal tars. From benzene came the first mauve dyes; from toluene chemists synthesized the indigo which makes blue jeans blue; phenols were crucial for the manufacture of aspirin, pesticides and phonograph records; anthracene was the base for alizarin dyes; naphthalene was transformed into antiseptics; cresols were used to make fumigating poisons.

It took the German genius for analysis and organization to unleash the full potential of the coal tars. During the 40 years of European peace following German unification (1871), no country in the world placed such emphasis on scientific research. Heidelburg and Freiburg were among the first universities to create academic laboratories and to preach the gospel of chemical progress. Few physical scientists anywhere were not trained in German universities or taught by someone who'd learned their art in Germany. Chemical production as we know it today — systematic, research-based, integrating theoretical science and practical engineering — was conceived and birthed by one German cartel: I.G. Farben. And the cornerstone of I.G. Farben was Bayer.

One of several Bayer emblems.

Unlike many corporate giants, the Bayer Company had no powerful, driven, aggressive founder. Friedrich Bayer opened his dye firm for business in 1863. Beginning with natural coloring agents, he and his partner, Johann Weskott, eased into the coal-tar dye market with fuchsin. Neither of the partners were particularly adept at organic chemistry or business. They depended on alizarin, an orange-red dye, for much of their trade. However, the market for alizarin weakened and the company faltered. If it weren't for the hiring of one man — Carl Duisberg — the firm would surely have failed, the 300 employees thrown into the street and the name Bayer relegated to footnotes of obscure chemical history books. Quickly, Duisberg developed a new method for making Congo Red dye, circumventing competitors' patents. Soon, he'd created two new dyes for Bayer, saving his employer from bankruptcy.

Carl Duisberg
(Courtesy of Bayer AG Archives)

No one person can be said to have presented heroin (and its little brother, aspirin) to the world. Various scientists, technicians, businessmen, and medical mercenaries had roles in the drama of heroin's birth. But it's safe to say that without Carl Duisberg, the drug would never have had the impact that it did. He didn't give birth to heroin, but he brought together the parents, consecrated their union, built the nursery, acted as the midwife and then blessed the birth as godfather.

A hundred years after heroin's birth, Carl Duisberg is largely forgotten. In his day, however, he stirred up the same fear, awe and envy as other commercial giants. Rockefeller, Ford, and Carnegie were his American counterparts. Born in 1861, he had little to look forward to in life besides perhaps taking over his father's modest ribbon-making business. But once he'd discovered chemistry, the trajectory of his life was unalterable. At age 22, he received his doctorate and began a research fellowship with Bayer and Company. In 1880, Friedrich Bayer died. The concern went public and the new director decided that fresh blood and new ideas were needed to get the company back in the black. Duisberg rose up the ladder quickly and was soon supervisor of research. By 1890, he'd taken over as de facto ruler of the entire company.

Heavy, florid in the face, with thinning hair and erect, waxed handlebar mustaches, he epitomized the successful man of business of his era. His broad, self-satisfied Prussian gloat left little doubt that here was a man intent on victory in all the commercial battles he fought. An unusual combination of Teutonic organizational fervor and scientific acumen, Duisberg transformed Bayer from an inconsequential dye firm into the most powerful chemical company in the world. Imperious and demanding, he thrust his hand into virtually every aspect of the company's operation. Memoranda in triplicate, meeting notes, research findings: all of these passed his desk for scrutiny. His Prussian zeal for order and authority were manifested in the "Führer principle," a term he used long before Hitler brought it to national consciousness. A pan-Germanic true believer, he was convinced that the "Fatherland" must strive to fulfill its destiny as the dominant power — both military and economic — of the 20th century. Though usually rigid and domineering, he could, when necessary, show great flexibility, flourishing under the Kaiser's rule, the Weimar Republic and the Third Reich.

Though Bayer remained a key player in the dye industry, Duisberg determined that the company needed to enter a new theater of operations. His competitors were already established in the pharmaceutical field. Kalle and company had been highly successful with a pain- and fever-reducing medicine they called Antifebrin. This drug may have been the first comprising of only one ingredient to be sold under a trademarked name, rather than by its generic chemical designation.

Duisberg learned that one of Bayer's thusfar useless by-products — paranitrophenol — was chemically similar to Antifebrin. Thousands of barrels of this residue were piled up in the factory yard, waiting for disposal. Duisberg ordered his researchers to find a way to create a new drug from these dregs.

Christening the new medication Phenacetin, and marketing it aggressively, Duisberg in effect reinvented the pharmaceutical industry. Phenacetin was the first drug ever to be created, manufactured, tested and sold all by the same commercial concern. Able to charge much more for the trademarked medicine, Duisberg infuriated pharmacists. However, by German law they were forbidden to dispense a generic drug if the prescription called for a specific product. Fate — in the form of an influenza epidemic which killed thousands in the U.S. and Europe — came to Bayer's aid. Phenacetin was prescribed by countless doctors, and the Bayer plant churned out tons of the pure white drug to meet the orders.

With these triumphs came the need for expansion. Bayer's laboratories were already too crowded. And Duisberg planned to hire more researchers to produce an even more varied line of chemical products.

Though he had, to a large extent, invented the modern commercial research lab, Duisberg's men worked in conditions that by current standards would seem ridiculously crude and chaotic. Lab tables were everywhere. Clouds of noxious vapors filled the air. Some researchers were forced to work in hallways, bathrooms, and unheated outbuildings. Some — who had no access to sinks — had no choice but to work by the river. The ground around the building was a caustic stew; men wore thick-soled wooden clogs because the mud would burn through leather shoes. Dogs roamed the laboratories, getting under the feet of the boys who scurried about collecting test tubes, beakers and bottles to be cleaned. Such was the chaos — and the spillage — that frequently a trail of footsteps, a rainbow brick road, led into town from the plant.

This clearly could not go on forever. Realizing the need for more order and more space (the dumping of toxic by-products was becoming a problem, too), Duisberg conceived of new research works which would set the standard for size, moderness and organization. Leverkusen was designed as the "perfect" industrial plant. It still stands, and operates according to Duisberg's original conception. Growth accelerated rapidly. Bayer employed a thousand men when Phenacetin was invented in 1888. Ten years later at heroin's nativity, the company had five times that many workers. At the beginning of World War One, Bayer was the biggest chemical concern in Germany, with over 10,000 employees.

The inventory of drugs that came from Bayer's Elberfeld and Leverkusen plants is impressive: the sedatives Sulfanol, Trional, and Veronal (a barbiturate), Hemicranin (for headaches), various preparations for tuberculosis, arthritis, insomnia and even a sugar substitute: Sycose. But surely the name Bayer will be forever associated with one much-beloved drug — aspirin — the most successful pharmaceutical ever created.

2.

Released to the public only a few months after heroin, created and tested in the same labs, goldmine and boon to millions of sufferers, aspirin and its invention can shine some light on heroin's origin.

Aspirin was the first mass market pain killer whose benefits were not outweighed by its drawbacks. The predecessors — Antifebrin, Antipyrine, Phenacetin — all had serious side effects. In large or extended dosage they caused the user's skin to turn blue (cyanosis) and killed red blood cells (methemoglobinemia). Severe stomach pains and a ringing in the ears were also common complaints. Finding a better analgesic would place Bayer in a very profitable position. Pain — Duisberg understood — can be lucrative. Whether the pangs of childbirth, the agony of surgery, or the more modest torments of headache, inflammation or arthritis, pain is a driving force behind medical innovation and pharmaceutical research. Both aspirin and heroin were Bayer's response to pain.

David B. Morris argues convincingly that our culture has embraced a "myth of the two pains": a belief that mental and physical pain are totally different phenomena. Common sense and enlightened science tell us that they, in fact, can not be separated. Pain, Morris writes, "is far more than simply or exclusively a medical problem. It can not be reduced to a mere transaction of the nervous system. The experience of pain is also shaped by such powerful cultural forces as gender, religion and social class."[1] If this seems unlikely, consider the medieval Catholic self-flagellator, the Iroquois warrior who defined his identity by his defiance of torture, the modern American evasion of the slightest discomfort. A culture's response to pain can tell us a great deal. A corporate or individual's attitude toward pain can be revealing also. Placing the control of pain entirely in the hands of medical experts, making a sharp distinction between "mental" and "physical" pain, using pain to fuel a profit-producing machine: these contributed as much to the invention of heroin as they did to aspirin.

Bayer and Company's response to pain.

The Birth of Heroin and
The Demonization of The Dope Fiend

More aspirin has been sold than any other analgesic. And a huge amount of it bore the well-known Bayer cross. Domestic, familiar, reassuring: aspirin followed one trajectory. Alien, threatening, eventually deemed demonic: heroin took the left-hand path. Both were pharmacological responses to pain. Neither was innocent of profit-motive or exploitation. Nor is either totally malign. It's difficult, perhaps impossible, to strip away 100 years of associations that have adhered like barnacles to the drugs' reputations. But in 1898, both were novel and untried. In fact, researchers treated aspirin with far more suspicion than heroin; it was thought to damage the heart, and remained on the shelf for months. It's important to keep in mind that both drugs entered the world the same way: trademarked, tested, manufactured and zealously protected as commercial property of Bayer and Company.

A number of legends and folkloric notions surround Bayer's most famous product. It was not — as some have claimed — actually discovered in the Elberfeld laboratory. It originated in crude form in the workshop of French chemist Charles Gerhardt. Sixteen years later, a German produced a purer form. The man associated with Bayer's aspirin — Felix Hoffman — found the formula in a book. However, he did devise a new method of synthesizing the drug, recording in his log that on October 10, 1897, he'd created a new process for converting salicylic acid into acetylsalicylic acid (a.k.a. aspirin).[2] Though it proved to be hugely successful, it was rejected at first by the Bayer testing staff. At this time — late 1898 — heroin was already on the market, selling well, collecting rave reviews from doctors and bouquets of praise from the first users. Aspirin had to wait until the next year, after finally getting the go-ahead from Heinrich Dreser, the head of testing. The name — unlike "heroin," which is rich in meanings — was a simple contraction of the German generic term: acetylspirsäure. In the summer of 1899, Dreser released aspirin for marketing. But at this time, the company didn't use direct consumer advertising. Bayer sent free samples to medical school faculties, hospital staff, and thousands of private physicians. Along with the drug came a request to publish any experimental findings. Ads were placed in medical journals. But aspirin's popularity was driven largely by word of mouth. By the end of the year, with aspirin's effectiveness established, its sales soared. Three years later, the medical literature on its uses and safety was enormous, and bright with praise.

Bayer had opened a gold mine; now its main task was to keep the claim jumpers away from the motherlode. Billions of aspirin tablets were purchased in the following 100 years. But at first, Bayer sold it in bulk-powder form to druggists, who pressed it into pills. This proved to be less profitable than having the Bayer logo on every tablet, and made it easier for patent pirates to cut into the market. Stamping the tablets with the now-familiar cross, along with continued vigorous promotion, helped establish the primacy of "pure" Bayer aspirin.

"The Bayer Bible" was Duisberg's next brain child. Starting in 1898, he had this weighty volume published and sent to every doctor in Germany. Inside were pseudo-objective descriptions of all medications then in use. But of course, Bayer products were heavily touted and the company name was placed prominently. This "holy book of healing" arrived just in time to promote Bayer's two newest products: aspirin and heroin. The campaign — along with circulars sent to 30,000 doctors inviting them to request free samples — was unprecedented, and extremely effective. Money poured in from Germany, Europe and around the world.[3]

Achieving near-hegemonic control, Duisberg set his sights even higher. His visionary ambition led not just to further research and aggressive marketing, but also to a new and unparalleled business organization: the creation of the largest, most powerful, and (many have said) most malign cartel in the world: I.G. Farben.[*]

---

[*] The name means literally "community of interests of colors."

3.

With a high altar in the paranoid's pantheon, I.G. Farben is one of the most hated, feared, envied and misunderstood business entities to ever exist. Conspiracy theorists have latched onto the I.G., seeing its sinister influence not only in the business world, but also in political machinations and social turmoil. Certain lawyers and scholars have spent their entire careers trying to untangle its knotted coils. Pictured often as a vast, sprawling octopus, with its slimy tentacles in everything from women's underwear to the depths of secret Swiss bank accounts, I.G. Farben achieved a near-mythic status. Some have argued that the cartel is so enormous, so complex, so deeply entrenched, that it can never be killed. Neither the Nuremberg tribunals (in which 24 of the I.G.'s top men were tried for Nazi war crimes), nor the power and determination of the victorious Allied occupation forces, could truly dismember this archetypal "thousand-limbed predator beast, this King Kraken with countless snaking arms, writhing in a fever of greed, deep in its lightless lair."[4]

As is usually the case with popular culture paranoia, there is truth mixed in with the outrageous beliefs. I.G. Farben was vast; it was deeply tied to the Nazi state; it had power greater than many national governments; and the major companies which came together in 1925 to form the cartel still live, in fact are thriving.

And from its labs come some of the most detested and terrifying substances known to mankind: heroin, chlorine and phosgene gases (the first poisons used in World War One), methadone (originally called

Dolophine), the death-camp toxin Zyclon-B, and the still-used military nerve gases: tabun and sarin.

Only five years after he shepherded heroin into the world, Carl Duisberg laid the plans for the most-reviled corporation in history. In 1903, he traveled to the U.S. to supervise the building of a Bayer aspirin and dye-stuff plant in Rensselaer, New York. The trip was less successful than he'd hoped; rival dye firms had hired private detectives to trail him from New York City up the Hudson River. But an unexpected result of his time in the U.S. was a rekindled admiration for the huge American trusts such as J.D. Rockefeller's Standard Oil of New Jersey. Despite formal anti-trust legislation, these immense industrial combines remained healthy and highly profitable. Rockefeller's monopolistic cartel had made him $500 million, largely by eliminating competition in the oil industry. Duisberg reasoned that he could do the same with the German chemical firms. Returning to Germany, he proposed to the "Big Six" dye-stuff makers (Basf, Bayer, Hoechst, Casella, Agfa, and Kalle) a combination of interests (Interessen Gemeinschaft).

In January of 1904, Duisberg drew up a 54-page plan to unite the sales, production, and research departments of the large chemical firms. This was not yet the "hundred-headed hydra" so feared by other companies. In the original memorandum, Duisberg proposed affiliation, but with a high level of autonomy for the firms. At the Kaiserhof hotel — the most ostentatious in Germany — Duisberg met with the directors of the other companies. Men of wealth and power, in formal attire, smoking expensive cigars and sipping the best cognac available, the stout gray-haired business lords gathered in conclave to plan. They came close to an agreement, but Hoeschst could not be convinced that uniting with Bayer would be in its best interest.

Within months, however, Hoechst had secretly combined with Casella to create their own I.G. Afraid that they'd be crushed by this combination, Bayer, Basf and Agfa united to form the Dreibund (or triple alliance). In 1915 — flush with profit from war production — Duisberg proposed that these two groups amalgamate to form a super-cartel. The companies agreed this time to coordinate research, marketing, manufacture and financial arrangements, but still each would retain its corporate identity.

The chaos following Germany's defeat — factories occupied by the Allies, patents lost, transport paralyzed — nearly destroyed the companies. Now chairman of the "Council of the Gods," the general board of I.G. Farben, Duisberg again pushed for a complete fusion. Desperate times forced the directors to consider more extreme measures. It took years of negotiation, but on September 15, 1925, the complete merger was sealed and I.G. Farben took its final form. Within a year, it was the largest company of any kind in Europe; only three worldwide were bigger.

Engorged with profit, the I.G. extended its tentacles farther and deeper. Hitler came to power in 1933, but well before that, Duisberg's brainchild was well enmeshed in Nazi plans. Crucial to the rearming of Germany — developing and making munitions, synthetic rubber and fuels for the burgeoning Wehrmacht — I. G. Farben made Hitler's design for European conquest possible. It's no exaggeration to say that without the I.G., he could not have begun the war, let alone come close to winning it.

Financially entangled with the rise of Hitler's Germany, the I.G. expanded. Millions of Deutschmarks flowed back and forth: political contributions one way and munitions contracts the other. Men served simultaneously in the Nazi Government and the I.G. leadership. Even before the war began, the total Nazification of the I.G. board was effected. All members who'd not yet joined the party did so in 1937, and all the Jews in official positions were removed.[5]

Perhaps most well-known and excoriated of the I.G.'s actions was the use of slave labor in its factories. Finding the administration of the main Auschwitz site not efficient enough, the I.G. set up its own satellite labor camp where thousands were worked to death. Even in the extermination chambers of the death camps Bayer's presence could be found. It was Bayer, in the same laboratory where aspirin and heroin were developed, that created the patent-protected essence of mass murder: Zyclon B.

Highly effective and highly profitable, Zyclon B was used for years as an industrial insecticide. By 1934, I.G. Farben had a worldwide monopoly on its distribution. Some confusion still surrounds the provenance of this exterminating agent because the Bayer name did not appear on the gas canisters. However, Josiah Dubois — prosecution chief for the War Crimes Tribunal which tried the I.G. Farben directors — states unequivocally that "every can of Zyclon B that went to Auschwitz through the firm of Tesch was produced by I.G. Farben Leverkusen."[6]

The labyrinthine structure of I.G. Farben makes it difficult to place blame on those ultimately responsible, but not impossible. I.G. Farben had a controlling interest in Degesh, which distributed the gas. Within the chemical industry it was an accepted fact that the I.G. and Degesh were indistinguishable; the smaller company proclaimed on its official communiqués that it was an exclusive sales agent for I.G. Farben. More damning, half the Degesh controlling board were I.G. Farben men. Wilhelm Mann, the chairman of Degesh (who'd joined the Nazi Party early in its history) had sat on the I.G.'s managing board since the mid-1930s. Such was the symbiotic relationship between the I.G. and Auschwitz that a teletype communication system was installed to connect the Bayer Leverkusen plant and the death camp.[7]

Odorless in its pure state, Zyclon B was too dangerous to sell as an insecticide without adding a foul-smelling chemical indicator. In fact, the patent for the compound (hydrocyanic or Prussic Acid) had expired years before. Thus, the only way Degesh could maintain its monopoly on the gas was through the warning scent.

When the S.S. began its human-extermination program, ranking officers demanded that the indicator be removed to ensure the efficiency of the gas chambers. Degesh demurred — to sell it in its pure form would open the company to competition. The S.S. men showed no tolerance for this petty concern for profit. They claimed a higher purpose than crass commercialism, and the gas was sold by the thousands of gallons without the added chemical. In 1943, Degesh had a remarkable increase in sales. Sixty-three percent of its business was in supplying Zyclon B to Auschwitz.[8] I.G. dividends from its Degesh holdings were double those of only three years before. Enough of the gas was shipped to kill 20,000,000 people.[9]

Insecticide for genocide — this is not such an incongruous use. If Jews were vermin — and Nazi propaganda repeatedly depicted them as such: dirty, malodorous, noxious, swarming, carrying some lethal contagion — then the use of pesticide was in keeping with the reigning ideology. Whether any of the men involved in this use of Zyclon B grasped this perverse connection is not known. But on Degesh procurement orders, it was baldly stated that the gas was to be used "to exterminate criminals, incurable patients and inferior human beings."[10]

Only the order-and-cleanliness-obsessed Germans could have conceived such an outrageous association: shower stalls as death chambers. But the Germans were certainly not the first to use "racial hygiene" ideology to such vile ends. It must be kept in mind that Auschwitz was not merely an extermination center; it was also an industrial complex employing slave labor. Just as the Nazis took American eugenics laws as their model (see Chapter Four, Section 4), so too their forced-labor program one-upped the American version. For centuries the U.S. used "subhumans" to drive its economy. Likewise, the Nazis enslaved thousands of Jews, Poles, Russians and Gypsies to keep the industrial machine humming. The concepts of "racial hygiene" and "protoplasmic purity," the exploitation of dark-skinned Others, find their ultimate expression in the I.G./Nazi death camps.

This was not, unfortunately, the first time Bayer's expertise served the purpose of mass murder. Thirty years before, on a battlefield in Belgium, a greenish-yellow fog drifted toward the Allied trenches. An artillery barrage had preceded the cloud. The French troops had survived those before. The cloud however, the first use of poisonous gas in World War One, was another matter. Liquid chlorine, stored in 5,000 metal cylinders, had been brought to the front the week before. At the opportune moment — 5 p.m. on April 22, 1915 — the canisters were cracked open and a deadly wall of chartreuse mist bore down on the French lines at Ypres. Five miles long, and as tall as a man, the cloud was inescapable and devastating. The chlorine reached the French, searing their eyes, burning like vaporous flames at the nose, mouth and throat. It left 15,000 causalities, one third of them dead. A gap four miles wide was ripped in the French lines. Only the unpreparedness of the German generals, who thought of this as a mere test and not of strategic importance, prevented the attack from becoming a disaster for the Allies.

As in Auschwitz, Leverkusen technology was at the heart of the slaughter. Carl Duisberg had seen in the early days of World War One that poisonous gases might be a boon to the military and a revitalizing shot in the arm for the floundering dye-stuffs industry. He was such a fervent believer that not only did he commit his laboratories to the project, but was also personally involved in the research. In the summer of 1915, Duisberg wrote glowingly to Major Max Bauer: "You should see what things look like here at Leverkusen, how the whole factory is turned upside down and reorganized so that it produces almost nothing but military contracts."[11]

Though the use of poison gasses did little to change the course of the war, the lessons of Ypres stayed with German military thinkers for decades. As the situation in Europe degenerated for the Nazis, upper-level officers pressured Hitler to use more advanced forms of poisonous gas on Russian and American strongholds. Code named, "N-stoff," the nerve gases tabun and sarin were discovered during I.G. Farben pesticide researches. They remained highly guarded secrets throughout the war. Though he thought it acceptable to use human subjects for testing — at concentration camps — Hitler was afraid that in the long run a nerve-gas attack would do more harm than good. The Allies had access to the same gases; I.G. Farben had patented both tabun and sarin in the late 1930s. Wounded in World War One, Hitler was haunted by the specter of escalating poison-gas warfare. In the end, his decision not to use the nerve gases was based on faulty understanding of his enemy's situation. In fact, the Allies had little in their arsenals to retaliate with.

The name sarin appeared again in the news years later when American troops destroyed poison gas stockpiles at the end of the Gulf War. It's thought that many were exposed to sarin, and this has been tentatively linked to the so-called Gulf War Syndrome. Apparently the ghost of I.G. Farben's chemical wizardry will not be laid to rest.

A final Bayer product should be mentioned before heroin's birth is treated in depth. As World War Two approached, German leaders feared a cut-off of opium supplies. Morphine would be in great demand as a painkiller for the wounded and maimed. And if the Allies created a blockade as they'd done in World War One, Germany's ability to treat its war casualties would be severely weakened. So the Bayer labs set to work creating a synthetic morphine substitute. Originally called dolophine, in honor of Adolf Hitler, it has since the war been marketed as methadone, and is used today as a maintenance drug to wean users away from heroin. It's apt, and no surprise, that Bayer should give the world its most feared drug and also then provide its most commonly used "cure." Profits accrue coming and going.

Notes:

1. Morris, David B. *The Culture of Pain.* (Berkeley: U. Cal. Press) 1991. p. 23.
2. Mann, Charles and Mark Plummer. *The Aspirin Wars.* (New York: Knopf) 1991.
3. *Ibid.*
4. Ellison, Richard. *The Beast: I.G. Farben.* (New York: Barret and Barret) 1979. p. 27.
5. Borkin, Joseph. *The Crime and Punishment of I.G. Farben.* (New York: Free Press) 1978. p. 72.
6. Dubois, Josiah. *Generals in Gray Suits.* (London: Bodley Head) 1953. p. 213.
7. *Ibid.,* p. 217.
8. *Ibid.,* p. 215.
9. *Ibid.,* p. 214.
10. *Ibid.,* p. 214
11. Borkin, Joseph. *The Crime and Punishment of I.G. Farben.* (New York: Free Press) 1978. p. 20.

Chapter Three
Virgin Birth

1.

There are two heroins: the chemical compound diacetylmorphine, and the trade-marked and heavily advertised, highly lucrative piece of merchandise that Bayer unveiled in 1898. Though identical chemically, the substance diacetylmorphine is profoundly different than "heroin." The first is largely unfamiliar. More significant, it is totally lacking in the extreme emotional content of the other. It's almost impossible now, 100 years after its birth, to say or write the word "heroin" without eliciting a violent — often irrational — response. Diacetylmorphine, on the other hand, is merely a clumsy chemical term. This point may seem a bit of sophistry, but it's crucial at the start of any discussion of heroin's actual entry into the world to keep in mind the freight cars of associations that heroin drags behind itself. "Heroin" as meant here is not merely one of many morphine derivatives, but a cultural essence. As the following pages will demonstrate, the drug has a status far beyond, and far more complex than, other opiate alkaloids. In short, heroin is a mythic force as much as it is a drug.

Though heroin was christened and given to the world in 1898, the chemical diacetylmorphine was actually stumbled upon almost a quarter of a century earlier. Heroin's nativity in the Bayer Elberfeld labs may be seen as the reincarnation of an avatar — returning to the world when the world was finally ready for it. It's no surprise that the creation of a substance so thoroughly demonized (after the medical world welcomed it with near-ecstatic praise) should be so mythologized.

This rebirth, this Second Coming of heroin, was quickly enveloped in a web of misconception. One of the most common — and most frequently repeated — fallacies is that heroin was invented and sold initially as a substitute for morphine, a tool for releasing morphinomaniacs from their chemical bondage. This, we'll see shortly, is patently untrue. The earliest research reports make no mention of substituting heroin for morphine. Another misconception is that Heinrich Dreser was the first to synthesize diacetylmorphine. Though Dreser was the crucial figure in Bayer's foray into opiate production and sales, he was preceded 24 years before by British chemist C.R.A. Wright as the actual discoverer of the drug.

Working at St. Mary's Hospital in London, Wright did extensive research into the chemical composition of certain natural and purified alkaloids. His experiments included boiling morphine on a stove with acetic anhydride, an acid closely related to ordinary household vinegar. One of the substances he created — in 1874 — was what Dreser came to name heroin.

F.M. Pierce, an associate at Owens College in London, performed the biological assays at Wright's request. Securing dogs with leather restraining harnesses, injecting with a solution of diacetylmorphine, Pierce was the first to see the effect of the new drug. He was disturbed by what he observed. The drug caused

> great prostration, fear and sleepiness following the administration, with the eyes being sensitive and pupils dilated, considerable salivation being produced in the dogs, and slight tendency to vomiting in some cases, but not actual emesis. Respiration was at first quickened, but

subsequently reduced, and the heart's action was diminished and rendered irregular. Marked want of coordinating power of the muscular movements and the loss of power in the pelvis and hind limbs, together with a diminution of temperature in the rectum of about four degrees, were the most noticeable effects.[1]

The publication of Wright's experimental findings elicited little response. Besides his article in the *Journal of Chemical Society,* the discovery went unremarked.

To what extent Wright's decision to forego further testing was affected by popular opinion is not clear. But there was already afoot in Britain a movement to drastically restrict opiate use. The Society for the Suppression of the Opium Trade was founded only a few months (November 1874) after Wright's experimental results were published. Though the Society focused at first on the Asian opium trade, its journal, *Friend of China,* devoted itself increasingly to articles about opiate use in general. It called for the prohibition of opiates except for medicinal uses, basing its argument on the belief that opium was "evil," could not be consumed in moderation, and was physically and morally destructive to the user.

The new substance languished in obscurity until 1890, when German chemist W. Dankwortt synthesized diacetylmorphine again. His work was valuable in that it provided greater understanding of the actual chemical composition of the drug. But as a commercial product, a medication, a force in popular culture, Dankwortt's creation was nothing.

Another eight years elapsed before the men at Bayer reincarnated diacetylmorphine as a drug: heroin.

2.

It was Heinrich Dreser who had the inspiration to test the drug on human respiratory disease. Dreser was a highly respected professor at the University of Bonn before he joined Bayer and became the head of the testing department at Elberfeld. With his shaggy, soup-strainer mustache, thinning hair, and intense scholarly scowl, he was the prototypical, zealot German scientist. Tiny, wire-framed glasses added to his fierce, rodent-like expression. Though hardly an Übermensch, Dreser exhibits, in some photos, the same wildman-prophet look as Friedrich Nietzsche.

At this time, the Bayer lab was divided into two sections: the pharmaceutical department, run by Arthur Eichengrün, and the testing department under Dreser's command. It's likely that heroin came directly from the testing section — as it had already been discovered and reported on, and Dreser was known to comb though research reports looking for orphan drugs which needed a good home. Dreser's genius — if that is the correct term — was like that of many other successful businessmen: the ability to exploit others' work, discovering applications for their basic research. As with the even more successful aspirin, Dreser had, however, more than a scientific interest in the new drug. He earned a substantial royalty on every medication that was marketed after testing in his lab. As an example of his self-aggrandizement, consider that he deemed aspirin too dangerous to merchandise at first. But when he was finally convinced by others' research, he published a scientific paper singing the praises of the new drug and neglecting to mention the two men who were instrumental in its development.

In 1898, Dreser's lab was considered one of the most modern in the world — with the best equipment and the brightest minds in the field. However, our notion of the high-tech lab is easily dispelled by a photo from the period, which shows a facility far different than the hermetically sealed "white room" of modern chemical research. Glowing gas lamps are suspended from rigid pipes above. Wooden tables more appropriate for the dining room than a modern lab are covered with a variety of apparatus: bulbous beakers, flasks, retorts. In the bottom corner of the picture, one of the many lab mascot dogs can be seen. And Dreser — master of this domain — sits among his men, like them dressed in frock coat, vest and tie. His posture is surprising similar to that of Thomas Edison in the famous "Five Day Vigil" photo. His arm rests heavily on the back of the chair, shoulders hunched and eyes slightly out of focus, the archetypal man of science exhausted by his heroic efforts.

Dreser performed the initial tests on Bayer employees. Then Dr. Floret moved on to phase two at the Elberfeld clinic. It's essential to keep in mind that heroin was conceived, tested, and marketed as a medication for respiratory diseases. Morphine had been used to treat tuberculosis, but doctors wanted a drug with fewer side effects. Heroin's birth announcement — Dreser's article in the *Therapeutische Monatschefte* — focused entirely on diseases of the lungs and respiratory passages. This might seem odd, or even ridiculous; heroin as a cough syrup? But at this time, respiratory diseases were the leading cause of death in Europe and America. The shadow of TB lay long and heavy over the industrialized world. In the mid-1800s, one in five persons died of this disease.[2] Though by the turn of the century TB (or consumption, or phthisis, as Dreser called it) was increasingly a disease of the poor, it was quite rightly feared by all. It struck with disregard for age or wealth; it killed city dwellers and rural populations with equal impunity. This so-called Great White Plague was the prototypical infectious killer of the 19th century; its preeminence left a lasting impact on medicine, popular notions of health and well-being, and the image of the human body.

Besides a battery of intensely painful systemic symptoms, the sense of suffocation and remorseless choking, as well as the exhaustion and convulsions of the lungs which struggled and failed to clear themselves of blood, pus and phlegm, made life with TB unbearable for many. A drug that could alleviate some portion of this suffering would obviously be very much in demand.

In the testing lab, Dreser began with small animals. Rabbits, guinea pigs and frogs were injected with heroin and then examined. In particular the volume of air intake and oxygen content of the blood were closely investigated. The injection of 10 mg. of heroin in the rabbit's bloodstream "clearly slowed its breathing." Dreser asserted in his report that — based on the rabbit test — heroin was far safer than codeine because "the lethal dose was 100 times the effective dose, whereas with codeine it was only 10 times the effective dose." Misuse of heroin — accidental or purposeful — was thus far less likely, he claimed. The rabbits which died in his experiments did so because of "respiratory paralysis."[3] Heart function and blood pressure — Dreser noted with satisfaction — were normal until the lungs seized up. Close examination of the hearts of heroin-injected frogs was also performed, and further comparisons to codeine were made.

Testing on humans produced similar promising results. Both Dreser and his colleague, Dr. Floret, prescribed heroin to workers at the Bayer plant. Dreser found heroin to be "highly effective in combating the illnesses of dozens of men." Common laborers, chemists' assistants, clerks, janitors, draymen and stationary engineers: anyone who suffered from a persistent cough was welcome to try the new drug free of cost. A wide variety of respiratory diseases were treated: catarrh (inflammation of the air passages), colds, bronchitis, phthisis, influenza. And in most cases, intractable and troubling coughs were much reduced.

His tests focused primarily on the amount of air which treated and untreated lungs could hold, and the oxygen content of the blood. Swollen and fluid-choked air passages were much improved by an injection of as little as 1 mg. of heroin. He found that in some cases the lung capacity of his subjects was doubled by a single dose.

Dreser's basic scientific argument was curious. He seemed to believe that heroin's primary effect was on the lungs and tracheal tissue, ignoring or not choosing to examine, systemic effects. His article is a perfect example of the scientist setting up an experiment — stacking the deck — to find exactly what he hoped to find. His logic seemed to follow this path: respiratory diseases were killing one out of five people, a hugely profitable market for a cough suppressant was waiting to be exploited, diacetylmorphine was available, morphine had been of some use in the past. Ergo: the new drug was a respiratory medication.

Heroin, according to Dreser, was a specific: a drug which affected only one condition or part of the body. He did display some passing concern for the patients' general well-being — mentioning that in high doses the breathing was considerably slowed — but moved on quickly after remarking that such dangerous doses were no longer used. Almost nothing was mentioned about side effects. Issues of dependence were glossed over. The effects on mental functioning were barely mentioned.

Dreser's method of testing his patients was to have them suck on graduated glass cylinders, drawing up measurable quantities of water. The picture one gets from his description is hardly the stereotypical heroin experience: an anteroom with long wooden benches where workers wait to see the doctor; stolid, hardworking German citizens whose coughing and hacking produce a constant din; one at a time they go into the inner examination chamber and place their mouths on the glass tubing and suck; then the doctor asks them to roll up their sleeves; he gives them a quick jab with the hypodermic needle and shortly the remorseless, clawing need to cough abates. Then the men are retested. Even in cases of very ill patients, there was a marked improvement in lung function. Dreser's article makes no mention of following the patient's progress over an extended period of time.

Pleased with the results, Dreser suggested that heroin be employed in a program of "preventive or protective therapy" to decrease the "air hunger" of those suffering from pneumonia. The new drug seemed perfectly safe, even for those patients who worked with heavy machinery or at complex mental tasks. There was, apparently, "no alteration of consciousness as is associated with sleep preparations."[4] For the treatment of so-called hectic fevers (a continual, wasting, febrile state common to TB patients), heroin also promised great relief.

Dreser concluded his article — which he presented at the 70th Congress of German Naturalists and Physicians at Dusseldorf — with the statement that Dr. Floret, to whom he passed the drug for further testing, discovered "the same completely satisfying results."[5]

Far less encumbered with ponderous scientific speculations than Dreser's article, Floret gives a surprisingly unvarnished glimpse into the minds and motivations of the testers at Elberfeld.

During the half year when I prescribed heroin at the walk-in clinic of the Elberfeld factory, the medication showed itself to be extraordinarily useful, prompt and reliable as a treatment for persistent coughs, as well as for chest pains and inflammation particular to the catahhr of both the upper and lower respiratory tracts (angina, pharyngitis, trachaeitis, bronchitis) in both the acute and more chronic forms. I treated approximately sixty patients with this preparation and they declared their agreement, that after taking the heroin powder, they felt an immediate improvement of their racking cough. And the chest and abdominal pains, when such difficulties occurred, also were reduced. "Doctor, the powder you prescribed worked so well that immediately after I took it I felt an improvement; the cough was much reduced by your powder." Such were the loud exclamations of praise that I heard frequently during my consulting hour. In several cases of year-long continuous coughing, caused by chronic bronchitis with emphysema, I obtained by the use of heroin in a week's time a lasting alleviation of the cough and thereby an improvement of the general state of health. One patient explained to me that up to now no medicine has worked so well as my powder. In the cases of bronchitis with a persistent cough, codeine in the usual doses was not able to provide substantial improvement; after taking a single dose of heroin, the patient felt great improvement in his condition. I had the opportunity to observe in myself the astonishingly quick action of heroin. A persistent hacking cough caused by inflammatory catahhr of my upper respiratory system which made my practice at the clinic difficult, particularly the violent attacks of coughing caused by the necessity of speaking frequently, was improved immediately by a single dose of 5 mg. of heroin, so that I could pursue my practice for many hours at a time without being troubled by coughs.

Likewise, I achieved, in the treatment of TB with heroin, very promising results. In the early stages as well as the advanced phases of the disease I obtained an improvement with heroin. In only four out of the approximately twenty-five cases of TB that I treated with heroin did I not obtain the desired results. In one of these cases I was, with morphine, also unable to produce any improvement; another patient I treated with codeine.

It appears that the difficulties of bronchial asthma were influenced quite favorably by heroin. In three of my patients the action was self-evident.

As a general pain-relieving medication, especially for troubles of the abdominal organs, it appears that heroin is not suitable.

Unfavorable secondary effects also appear not
to be associated with the medication. Nausea,
vomiting, constipation, loss of appetite, etc. which
are frequently observed with morphine use, were
not found with heroin. Only one patient indicated
that after taking the powder, he experienced sudden dizzyness.

The preparation was moreover very well toler-
ated. The patients who were able to bear the fundamental burden of work carried on under the effect of the medication unhampered. A habituation
to the drug appears not to occur.[6]

Here then, we have the first endorsement of heroin:
safe, effective, with few side effects and — according to
Floret — no tendency to cause habituation. The term
"addiction" never once appears, and the notion of
"addiction" as it came to be understood later is likewise
nowhere to be seen.

3.

Why Bayer decided to name its new drug "heroin" is a question that may never be answered definitively. The reason most commonly given is that some of Dreser and Floret's patients claimed that when they were using heroin they felt *heroisch* (heroic). Used this way, the German term has a slightly arcane or pedantic flavor; an English equivalent might be "Herculean" or "Jasonic." By injection, in powder form, and mixed with water in drops, heroin was used on nearly 100 men at the Elberfeld plant. According to the frequently repeated tale, a sense of elation, release, and power transformed the men from ordinary workers into "heroes." Though this explanation has been repeated by many so-called experts in the field, there are obvious flaws. First-time users of heroin are likely to describe the effect of the drug as an all-pervading warmth, a sense of great peace and total well-being. This does not jibe with the active, larger-than-life associations we have with the word "heroic." If it were cocaine or amphetamines that Dreser used, perhaps this explanation would carry more weight. Dreser and Floret wrote about the absence of pain, not the sudden presence of new energy and virile strength.

The earliest version of this folkloric explanation comes from Richmond Pearson Hobson, whose career as the "Father of the Dope Fiend" I'll discuss at some length in Chapter Five. In an interview given to *The Saturday Evening Post*, Hobson claimed that the first heroin user

> experienced an exaltation of consciousness in which he imagined himself capable of heroic action. To him nothing seemed impossible. Rather, he be-

lieved himself immune from all possibility of failure. The more difficult or dangerous the task to which his excited brain prompted him, the more certain he was of easy accomplishment.[7]

The interview is rife with factual errors and bizarre statements: "the upper cerebral regions (contain) the shrine of the soul;" "narcotic tablets were being enclosed in hot-dog sandwiches and ice cream cones;" "religious conversation may as yet be considered the advanced addict's only hope of freedom."[8] In this context, his unsubstantiated claims regarding the term "heroin" are highly suspect.

A more likely way of accounting for the term is that it derives from a slightly different interpretation of *heroisch*. In German medical terminology of the day, the word meant large, extreme, unusually powerful, and implied a therapeutic effect that was strong even if prescribed in small doses. This is valid, as far as it goes, but incomplete in explaining the origin of the name. To find the true roots of the term, we need to go back to the first decade of the 19th century, when "heroic therapy" was one of the reigning medical ideologies. The term could not have been unknown to Dr. Dreser. This would be like a psychiatrist in the 1950s professing ignorance of Freud's theories. As late as 1879, Dr. J.B. Mattison was recommending a "heroic plan" of assault on patients' bodies.[9] Discussing the overuse of chloral hydrate, he argued that the "heroic" application of morphine and codeine could be highly effective. As one of the most pervasive and influential systems of medical thought in the 1800s, heroic therapy — the name and the concept behind it — likely influenced the christening of Bayer's new product.

Dr. Benjamin Rush, advocate of "heroic therapy"
in the 19th century.
(Courtesy of Dictionary of American Portraits)

Heroic therapy reached its apotheosis in the work of Dr. Benjamin Rush. A signer of the Declaration of Independence, founder of the first medical school in the U.S., undisputed father of American psychiatry, Rush casts a very long shadow over 19th century medicine. In his practice, massive and at times life-threatening remedies were inflicted on the patient. The usefulness of this therapy was — according to Rush — in direct proportion to its impact on the body. So, repeated and copious bleedings, the dosing with mercurious chloride (calomel) until the mouth hemorrhaged, intestinal purges that left the patient prostrate with exhaustion, blisters and cupping were performed with the ferocity, a single-minded devotion, only matched by a high-church inquisitor. In heroic therapy, the physician was the hero; the scalpel was his saber and the patient his battlefield. With manly strength and aggression, the practitioner of Rush's system of therapy was obligated to attack disease. Rush argued that the body must be thoroughly "depleted" before healing could begin. Thus, venesection was applied to cure the pains of childbirth; unfortunately, the heavy loss of blood would often push the woman into unconsciousness.

For Rush and numerous acolytes, pain itself was disease. And basing his theory on John Hunter's concept of counter-irritation, Rush claimed that the body can only be afflicted by one disease at a time. If pain were a disease, then excruciating pain could drive out other life-threatening maladies. Similarities to exorcism are obvious: an alien force was thought to invade the sanctity of the body, an expert (usually a man with great personal power and institutional backing) was brought in to loose an overwhelming attack on the affliction. The body was merely a stage on which the warlike drama was enacted.

Rush exhorted his followers to see themselves as heroic, bold, courageous, hyper-masculine, even patriotic as they inflicted agonies on their patients. He even discussed such novel therapies as whipping and the application of red-hot irons to cure poisoning. One of his devotees, John King, recommended the "bastinadoing of the soles of the feet" as a cure for labor pains.[10]

These ideas — though now we might consider them absurd and sadistic — were not the perverse power fantasies of a few extremists. They reflect a belief common at this time: the pain must be present for healing to occur. Rush's doctrine was built on the cultural notion that anything gained without suffering was of little value. Though medicine may be the field where this is best demonstrated, other professions evidenced a similar obsession with pain. Teachers beat their students with a grim glee; judges sentenced law-breakers to torture and death for crimes we now consider trivial; priests inflicted penances; and dentists operated on wailing and writhing patients. Pain, to a large degree, was at the heart of many 19th century professions. The grudging acceptance of anesthetics, and the open hostility to pain-free medicine, reflect not unthinking sadism, but a pervasive philosophical stance. Though by the time heroin was introduced, anesthetics and a certain liberalizing attitude competed with the brutality and cruelty of many professions, pain was still often seen as necessary for the greater good.

What then might Dreser and Duisberg have been thinking when they applied the term *heroisch* to a drug that came to be known as the pain-killer without equal? It's very unlikely that they thought in terms of clever inversions of cultural meanings, a turning inside-out of expectations. These were not post-modern deconstructionists, not even modern ironists. They were men devoted to business, profit, and the expansion of German economic power.

Heroin was used to combat the most lethal disease in the industrialized world. If illness was disorder, then a drug such as this was a powerful instrument for re-establishing order. The name "heroin" may not have been an inversion of the late 19th century ideology of pain, but an extension of it, a pushing to the logical extreme. Heroin as therapy was effective, overwhelming at times, almost instantaneous. Did Dreser and Duisberg understand how powerful the drug was when they named it? They were certainly aware of C.R.A. Wright's original ex-

periments and his reluctance to go further with diacetylmorphine. They saw the immediate effects of heroin
on their patients at the Elberfeld clinic. They came to
understand that heroin's impact was four to eight times
greater than that of morphine. And unlike the other
Bayer pharmaceuticals of the time, the new drug was not
given a bland, symptom-specific name such as Antifebrin, or an innocuous, generic name such as Veronal or
Trional. Heroin was — whether Dreser and Duisberg
were conscious of it — a response to pain, a triumph
over pain, a heroic assault on pain.

4.

Probably no remedy was heralded so enthusi-astically as was heroin. The prominent place held by opium derivatives in therapeutics, the constant calls on every physician to relieve pain and induce sleep with drugs, and the relative inadequacy of all substitutes for opium combined from the outset to stimulate the use of heroin. It was apparently the ideal preparation — potent analgesic and sedative — at the same time possessing other qualities highly desirable in certain ailments, above all free-dom from the dreaded so-called "habit-forming" qualities of the parent drug.[11]

This was the opinion of Charles Terry and Mildred Pellens, argued in great detail in *The Opium Problem,* the most thorough study of early 20th century opiate use yet written. Just as significant as their exhaustive research is the fact that at the time the book was written — the mid-1920s — the cultural attitudes about opiates, the mono-lithic medical mythos surrounding drugs, had not yet crystallized. The authors certainly do have an agenda, a therapeutic theory they wish to promote, but it isn't the generic mantra-like "truths" so often chanted in books about "addiction."

Terry's theories of opiate use will be treated in a later chapter. It's sufficient here to state that as a lifelong pub-lic-health worker — actually engaging with the popula-tion he was paid to serve, rather than promulgating theories from on high — Terry developed a somewhat more realistic understanding of opiate use than the paternalistic, liberal reformers or the hard-nosed, conservative law-and-order man.

The Opium Problem is indispensable for tracing the trajectory of response which the medical profession gave to Bayer's new drug. Heroin's later demonization could only have occurred if it were first praised as a nearly-miraculous panacea.

Dr. G. Strube appears to be the first researcher to publish findings after the initial work at Elberfeld. He tested heroin on 50 TB patients at the Medical University of Berlin, and observing the effects, stated:

> the patients took the medication willingly and habitués were satisfied with the exchange. Many, in whose case it was given under proper indications, asked for it again, if it was replaced by some other drug such as codeine. Whether this gives the first sign of habituation to the drug I can not decide with certainty, but this is possible since with patients who took it over a long period, I had to gradually increase the dosage to obtain the same results. From its considerable narcotic action and the inclination of the patients to use it again, I have deemed it advisable to use it only under strict control and not too freely, so that its beneficial action will not be discredited through abuse and indolence.[12]

In two articles (1898 and 1900), Dr. Manges reported on the treatment of tubercular and asthmatic coughs. Reviewing 341 cases of heroin use, he claimed that habituation to the drug was only a minor concern. Only 6-8% of the patients became "heroinists" and all "without the bad effects accompanying the morphine habit." His recommendation that heroin be used to break the morphine habit is likely the first in print.

Terry and Pellens cite six medical reports from 1899 which promote the use of heroin, and either make no mention of dangerous side effects or state directly that it does not lead to tolerance.

Dr. Turnauer in the same year, also reported on the tests he made to determine the possible harm heroin might cause. In some of the 48 cases of respiratory disease he noted a tolerance to the drug; the dosage was increased in almost all the patients. Still, he believed that there were "no harmful results, especially as I observed no abstinence symptoms whatever."

Allowing some time to elapse appeared to lessen the tolerance considerably.

In any event, from this as well as from my observation, it may be concluded that, regarding tolerance to heroin, certain individuals react peculiarly and it is recommended that in the case of the old and feeble persons, the initial dose should not be above .005. Heroin was found to be in general a harmless drug, which in most cases, even in patients accustomed to narcotics, can be used with success treating coughs and forms in this connection a valuable addition to our therapeutic agents.[13]

Reception in the English-speaking world was equally positive. Dreser's discovery was mentioned in the November 1898 issue of *The Journal of the American Medical Association*. *Lancet*, in Great Britain, a month later, also sang heroin's praises. The new drug was "a favorable substitute for morphine by not altering the blood pressure and thus to be well borne by persons of a weak heart and feeble arterial system." It was free of harmful secondary effects and could be administered "in comparatively large doses with no side effect but that of a sedative on the air passages."[14] Horatio Wood, in *Merck's Archive*, added his voice to the chorus of adulation, though he noted that heroin must be given in increasing doses to maintain its effect. Terry and Pellens cite over a dozen American studies from 1900 to 1901 which reported favorably on heroin — for coughs, as an analgesic, and as a sedative. A number of these researchers stated unequivocally that no habituation occurred with the use of heroin.

In the five years after heroin's introduction, most reports were highly favorable. There was a minority, however, which warned against the new drug. It appears that Harnack, in 1899, was the first to draw attention to heroin's negative effects. In his article "Regarding the Poisonous Nature of Heroin" he stated that the drug was dangerous if "placed in the hands of unsuspecting physicians."[15] Morel-Lavalleé echoed the warning three years later, though in less urgent terms, and still recommended heroin as an effective pain-killer for incurable diseases. It was, he claimed, superior to morphine because it did not cause euphoria.

Beside these few scattered nay-sayers, the medical profession's response was a loud and emphatic "yes" to heroin. Here was a medication which would solve a vast array of problems. Even two decades after heroin was introduced, when evidence of tolerance and dependence was mounting, many doctors continued to count on the drug. J.D. Trawick, for instance, expressed his attachment in homey terms: "I feel that bringing charges against heroin is almost like questioning the fidelity of a good friend. I have used it with good results, and I have gotten some bad results, such as a peculiar band-like feeling around the head, dizziness, etc., but in some cases referred to, it has been almost uniformly satisfactory."[16]

By 1906, heroin was well enough established that the American Medical Association's Council on Pharmacy and Chemistry included it in the annual "New and Nonofficial Remedies" listing. "When given in small doses, heroin hydrochloride has apparently no effect on any of the vital functions except respiration." Though it was habit-forming, heroin was nonetheless recommended for the treatment of respiratory illnesses. "It has also been recommended as an analgesic, in the place of morphine in various painful affections."[17] The same year, Squibb's *Materia Medica* listed it as a "remedy of much value. It is also used as a mild anodyne and as a substitute for morphine combating the morphine habit."[18]

Here we see the first steps in heroin's transformation. As questions rose regarding its use as a cough suppressant, doctors began to see heroin in a new light; within eight years of its release, it was widely and officially promoted as a "cure" for morphinism. The actual substance of course remained the same; but the drug's status, its use within the medical world, and soon its reputation in the legal realm, was rapidly changing.

Repeatedly in the history of technology we can find examples of innovative processes or inventions being freighted with importance far beyond their practical uses. Again and again (e.g. steam power, electricity, internal combustion engines, radio, TV, computers), new technologies serve a cultural totemic function, as objects onto which we can project our fears, hopes, wishes and desires. Like the totem animal of many tribal societies, the new invention becomes larger than life, vaguely supernatural, or a savior. Heroin is a perfect example of this phenomenon: a potent, intriguing new substance which was given a role beyond simple therapeutics. Because of its great power, heroin more than any drug before became a focal point, attracting a swirling cloud of inchoate cultural forces, just as a lightning rod attracts and redirects the huge and potentially dangerous static electricity generated by clashing storm clouds.

In a 1902 review of current research, J.L. Jarrige pointed to the numerous doctors who were already promoting heroin as a substitute for morphine. He quotes Morel-Lavalleé ("I consider heroin as an admirable medicine from many points of view even if we did not hope through it to some day witness the end of morphinism") as an example of the widely held notion that heroin was an effective "demorphinizing agent."[19]

To this day, many well-regarded academics and so-called drug-abuse experts accept and espouse the belief that heroin was created expressly as a substitute for morphine. This, we've seen, is patently untrue. Early on, heroin was touted as a replacement for morphine in the treatment of respiratory disease. But if the word "substitute" is used to mean an agent of cure, a tool to wean users off morphine, then the term is only accurate in a small number of later cases.

The continued acceptance of this "mythological explanation of heroin's birth"[20] is a useful point of entry into one wing of the huge edifice that "addiction theory" has become. John Kramer argues that heroin's birth was reconfigured by various anti-narcotics crusaders who sought to push the nation and Congress to support narcotic control legislation. In part they did this by exaggerating certain data and distorting reports regarding addiction. Among the myths they created was the depiction of all opiates as the "Demon Flower." In particular heroin was painted as a special evil. The frequency of its use as a substitute for withdrawal was exaggerated far out of proportion to the facts.[21]

As is often the case, a story told often enough is accepted as fact. Repeated over the years in print and in anti-narcotic speechifying, the story was accepted both in popular belief and by self-appointed authorities in the field.

5.

After Bayer inundated the German medical profession with its "Bible" and offered free samples of the new drug, it advertised heroin in a variety of languages: English, Russian, French and Italian. Magazine ads from the period show the family of Bayer drugs, aspirin and heroin featured prominently.

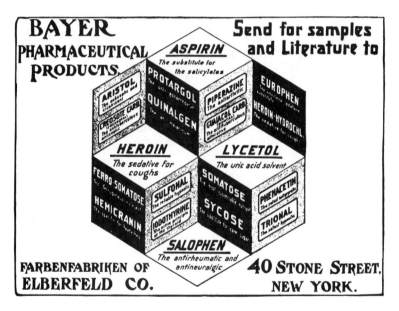

The Bayer family of products.

For 16 years after its introduction, heroin was widely and easily available: over the counter in drug and grocery stores, and by mail order. It's difficult for us now to imagine going to the neighborhood pharmacy or food shop and asking for a packet of heroin as we would ask for toothpaste or mouthwash. But throughout Europe and America this was exactly the case: self-diagnosis and self-medication. As Americans had dosed themselves with morphine and opium for a variety of ailments, so they continued with heroin. The notion of "drug habit" was familiar to the average American, but even at its worst, it was considered a social embarrassment, a vexing annoyance. If the medicine remained freely available, cheap and untainted ("Trust the Bayer Company for Pure Pharmaceutical Products") then it was much preferable to a slow, hacking death by TB or pneumonia.

The actual volume of heroin which Bayer produced and sold will likely never be determined. Likewise, the extent of the profits which accrued because of the new drug will also remain unknown. Trademark infringement and pirating were common. Other pharmaceutical companies entered the market; heroin is relatively easy to synthesize. For our purposes at this point, it's sufficient to state that heroin was well-trusted, dependable, inexpensive and widely accepted.

Why then did it become America's most demonized substance? Why did it take the paramount position — above plutonium, dioxin, LSD, crack, nuclear fallout — in the list of substances most hated and feared by Americans? The answer lies in the complex interplay of purity and pollution, in the values, ideals, beliefs, traditions and social needs which dominated the American psyche in the early 20th century.

Notes:

1. Wright, C.R.A. "On the Action of Organic Acids and Their Anhydrides on the Natural Alkaloids." *Journal of the Chemical Society.* (12) July 1874. p. 1031.
2. Rothman, Sheila. *Living in the Shadow of Death.* (New York: HarperCollins) 1994. p. 2.
3. Dreser, Heinrich. "Pharmakologisches über Einige Morphinderivate." *Therapeutische Monatschefte.* 12 (1898) p. 509.
4. *Ibid.,* p. 511.
5. *Ibid.,* p. 511.
6. Floret, Adolf. "Klinische Versuche über die Wirkung und Anwendung des Heroins." *Therapeutische Monatschefte.* 12 (1898) p. 512.
7. Hobson, Richmond P. "Heroin Heroes." *Saturday Evening Post.* September 20, 1924. p. 41.
8. *Ibid.,* p. 42.
9. Mattison, Jansen. "Chloral Inebriety." New York Academy of Medicine Pamphlette #1811. 1879. n.p.
10. King, John. *Eclectic Obstetrics.* n.p.
11. Terry, Charles and Mildred Pellens. *The Opium Problem.* (New York: Committee on Drug Addictions) 1928. pp. 76-77.
12. *Ibid.,* p. 77.
13. *Ibid.,* p. 79.
14. *Lancet* 2. December 3, 1898. p. 1511.
15. Terry, Charles and Mildred Pellens. *The Opium Problem.* (New York: Committee on Drug Addictions) 1928. p. 79.
16. Trawick, John. "A Case of Heroin Poisoning." *Kentucky Medical Journal* (9) p. 187.

17. Terry, Charles and Mildred Pellens. *The Opium Problem.* (New York: Committee on Drug Addictions) 1928. p. 84.
18. Szasz, Thomas. *Ceremonial Chemistry.* (New York: Doubleday) 1974. p. 195.
19. Terry, Charles and Mildred Pellens. *The Opium Problem.* (New York: Committee on Drug Addictions) 1928. p. 82.
20. Trebach, Arnold. *The Heroin Solution.* (Yale U.P.) 1982. p. 41.
21. *Ibid.,* p. 41.

Chapter Four
Demonization

1.

The decline and fall of heroin closely parallels the rise to national prominence of the American Cult of Purity. In the decades between the Chinese Exclusion Act of 1882 and the repeal of Prohibition in 1934, the U.S. was gripped by the increasingly feverish hand of hysteria, paranoia and xenophobia. All that was deemed alien to American ways, all that seemed a threat to traditional social order, was targeted for elimination. The Chronology of this book (pages 219 through 221) contains a year-by-year outline of the period. Here, it's sufficient to mention a few of the landmarks in this national hygienic upheaval and to point out that they were all built on the same foundation, that particularly American obsession with purity: physical, psychic, sexual and social.

Alien immigration (especially from Asia) was perceived as a threat to social order, and numerous efforts were made to stem it. The eugenics movement rose to national prominence during this period (reaching its peak in the mania for mass sterilization that gripped both Germany and the U.S.). The female body was subjected to an all-out assault by the medical profession — roughly 150,000 ovaries were "extirpated" in hopes of cleansing woman-kind of its biological taint.[1] Also, this time was known as the "Golden Age of Clitoral Excision," as woman's sexual nature was targeted as a threat to social order. Purity groups such as the American Society of Sanitary and Moral Prophylaxis sprang up all over the U.S. Various national laws — the Pure Food and Drug Act, the Mann Act to limit the "white slave trade," the Harrison Anti-Narcotic Act, sterilization laws, Prohibition, legal requirements for loyalty oaths — were created to maintain the sanctity of the national soul. The KKK was reborn, and the American Legion formed, both largely as a response to foreign "infectious" influences on the American body politic. The Carnegie Institution began the radical restructuring of public education. The Red Scare of 1919 came close to paralyzing the nation. The Federal Bureau of Narcotics was formed. The list goes on and on. But all have in common an underlying dread of disorder and impurity. A horde of secretive, alien forces was felt to be contaminating the pure essence of American culture; only vigorous and at times violent responses could maintain the essential goodness, even godliness of the U.S.A.

The extreme hostility toward heroin and the attendant creation of the popular cultural figure who came to be known as the Dope Fiend are a direct result of — one might say the crowning achievement of — America's hysterical fears and resentments.

2.

It's impossible to truly understand heroin's preeminence in American demonology (and the looming of the Dope Fiend over the psychic landscape) without first understanding the evolution of American attitudes toward dirt, disease and contagion. The Dope Fiend and his archetypal instrument of defilement — the hypodermic syringe — did not spring full-blown from the foreheads of American doctors and lawmen in the early 1900s. A paragon of filth, sexual menace, and irrational violence and crime, the Dope Fiend was and is a paranoid fantasy that feeds on the fears of white, middle-class America. He is as much a mythic figure as the cowboy, gangster, or rugged pioneer. He has ancestors in popular consciousness that can be traced as far back as the first colonists in the New World.

Cotton Mather, Avatar of American Puritanism.
(Courtesy of Dictionary of American Portraits)

The great Puritan divine Cotton Mather used the term "Wars of the Lord" to describe the difficulties the colonists encountered. He pictured the church in New England as a chaste "maid, sitting in a wilderness, compassed about by hungry lions, wolves, boars and bears and all manner of cruel and hurtful beasts, and in the midst of many furious men assaulting her every moment."[2] In other words, the Puritan church was a beautiful virgin, untouched, undefiled by animal instincts or desires, in a state of constant sexual peril.

Landing in the New World, the Puritans found native inhabitants whom they quickly invested with Old World fears and guilts, making them part of the New World mythos. Not just subhuman creatures, the Indians were embodiments of bestial impulses, even agents of Satan himself (whom we'll encounter again ruling over a horde of Dope Fiends). Cotton Mather used terms such as "tawnies," "wild beasts," "blood hounds," "jackals," "rattlesnakes," and "infidels" to describe the Indians. And he praised God for using disease (most likely smallpox) to "cleanse" the land of heathen taint:

> The indians in these Parts had nearly, Even about a Year or Two before, been visited with such a prodigious Pestilence: as carried away not a tenth, but Nine parts of Ten (yea 'tis said Nineteen of Twenty) among them: so that the woods were almost cleared of these Pernicious Creatures to make Room for better Growth.[3]

Disease was not only a weapon in God's arsenal — beating back the foes of the True Church — but Divine Punishment. "Sickness is in fact *Flagellum Dei Pro Peccatis Mundi*" (the whip of God for the sins of the world),

Mather exclaims in *The Angel of Bethesda*, reminding the elect that they were tainted by Adam's fall. The poison of the "old serpent" infected even newborn babies. Plagues and poxes could be seen as outward signs of inward corruption.

Though Puritan thought had a major shaping influence on later American attitudes regarding dirt, disorder and disease, Mather's relationship with actual human ordure was not the arch-American "cleanliness is godliness" ideal. For instance, he recommended the ingestion of feces and urine as medicine. "Human excreta is a remedy for Human Bodies hardly to be paralleled... and urine has virtues far beyond all water of medicinal springs."[4]

Mather has been called the "first significant figure in American medicine,"[5] uniting religious and medical philosophy. Thus he's a fitting figure to begin with when tracing American notions of purity (physical as well as moral). Though much of his medical theory was repudiated, still his association of sin and disease foreshadows later American beliefs regarding hygiene.

The hoary adage "cleanliness is next to godliness" was resurrected by evangelist John Wesley and preached from a thousand pulpits. And though Americans were by all accounts far dirtier in the 18th century than their European cousins, the *idea* of cleanliness was a huge importance, finding "ritual incantation" in the works of Wesley, Benjamin Franklin, Benjamin Rush and other shapers of the American mind.[6] In a land where daily bathing was almost unheard of (and in fact was thought of as a kind of perversion by many), where the streets were piled with great steaming heaps of human and animal excreta, where soap and water were luxuries few could afford, the equation of cleanliness and godliness may seem odd. But Americans have, since earliest colonial days, been a people obsessed with ritual purity and defilement.

John Wesley, American clergyman who popularized the phrase,
"Cleanliness is next to godliness."
(Courtesy of Dictionary of American Portraits)

Benjamin Franklin railed against uncleanliness.
(Courtesy of Dictionary of American Portraits)

Franklin, in his autobiography, listed 13 virtues, among them "cleanliness," and exhorted his readers to "tolerate no uncleanliness in body, clothes or habitation."[7]

By the early 1800s, inner and outer cleanliness were thought to be inextricably linked. Cleanliness in fact symbolized a state of moral wholeness and mental wellbeing. Benjamin Rush was much enamored with John Wesley's work and extolled cleanliness as "a physical means of promoting virtue."[8] Even the Salvation Army, founded by William and Catherine Booth in 1865, was built on the slogan "Soap, soup, and Salvation."[9] Street corner brass bands, snappy military uniforms, the gospel: none of these were effective if the sinner's physical form remained dirty.

Henry Ward Beecher proclaimed that clergymen could, in good conscience, recommend soap to sinners.
(Courtesy of Dictionary of American Portraits.)

Evangelist Henry Ward Beecher took this idea to its absurd Victorian extreme, appearing in a Pear's soap ad, proclaiming that "if cleanliness is next to godliness, Soap must be considered as a means of Grace and a clergyman who recommends moral things should be willing to recommend soap."[10]

Repeatedly, men and women steeped in fervent Protestant beliefs came to the forefront of the hygienic movement, and led the forces of cleanliness into battle. Just as eugenics, working toward "protoplasmic purity," was deeply affected by evangelical beliefs and motives, so too did public health proponents build their arguments on a charismatic foundation. The voices calling for reform in the disposal of human and animal filth, pure drinking water, housing and tenement improvement, and safe city sewerage were all led by evangelicals.

John H. Griscom — an important leader of the movement — summed up the attitude and echoed at the same time Cotton Mather's correlation of sin and disease. "The coincidence, or parallelism, of moral degradation and physical disease, is plainly apparent to any experienced observer."[11]

It's in the rise of America's temperance crusade that various elements come together and set the stage for the demonization of opiates. Sin and disease, evangelical fervor, the obsession with bodily defilement, the image of Women as agent of moral purification: all of these are linked in the anti-liquor juggernaut that rolled across American society. The Women's Christian Temperance Union was founded in 1874 and thousands of its foot soldiers — wearing white ribbons as symbols of purity — marched, preached and wielded hand-axes against the Demon Rum. The Anti-Saloon League, formed 1893, carried the crusade deeper into the heart of enemy territory.

Elizabeth Cady Stanton, influential Suffragette,
detested alcohol, calling it "unclean."
(Courtesy of Dictionary of American Portraits, above and below)

Susan B. Anthony, Suffragette leader, also detested alcohol.

Alcohol was not merely inebriating. It was "the unclean thing," declared Elizabeth Cady Stanton in 1852; "to taste, see, smell or touch it, polluted female Virtue as contact with Pork pollutes a follower of Mosaic law."[12] Sister suffragist Susan B. Anthony proclaimed "...speed the day when no young man who pollutes his lips with the drunkard's cup shall presume to seek the favors of our precious daughters."[13] Vessels of purity, undefiled by liquor, libido or lack of bathing, the idealized Woman was the last bastion of God's pure creation. Sexual boycotts were even proposed; to marry a man who drank at all would pollute any "precious daughter." "Lips that Touch Liquor Must Never Touch Mine," a song from this period, sums up the hysterical correlation of Demon Rum and damnation:

> *O John! how it crushed me, when first in your face*
> *The pen of the "Rum Fiend" had written "disgrace";*
> *And turned me in silence and tears from that breath*
> *All poisoned and foul from the chalice of death.*
> *It scattered the hopes I had treasured to last;*
> *It darkened the future and clouded the past;*
> *It shattered my idol, and ruined the shrine,*
> *For lips that touch liquor must never touch mine.*[14]

The differences between sanitation and salvation were blurred and then erased in this "most pervasive social reform movement in American evangelical history."[15] In the battle against the bottle, most of the themes sounded later in the so-called War on Drugs are present.

Carry Nation is likely the figure who will always be most closely associated with the temperance movement. Her "hatchetations" and withering school-marm scowl are the stuff of popular legend. What's less well-known is the fact that she saw herself in overtly prophetic terms, a modern-day version of Jeremiah, or even Jesus cleansing the temple. Her career as a saloon smasher began with a "murmuring musical" voice "which seemed to be speaking in her heart."[16] It instructed her to prepare weapons and begin her assault, not just on alcohol, but against the evil national institutions which supported the "liquor plague." In her vision, she saw the president of the U.S. toppled from a throne just as Old Testament prophets foresaw the downfall of once and future tyrants.

Carry Nation, Temperance zealot extraordinaire!
(*Courtesy of Dictionary of American Portraits*)

This was in 1899. At the same time, all over the country men and women were forming militant groups to combat the perceived invasion of depravity. Cotton Mather had founded the first American purity organization, the Society for the Suppression of Disorder, to shut down all of Boston's brothels. As the 20th century opened, purity crusaders were gathering their forces, beating drums, and beating plowshares into spears. This was war. Anthony Comstock's Society for the Suppression of Vice, the Anti-Saloon League, and the America Purity Alliance were eager to take on immorality in any form: liquor, impure speech or writing, birth control, the "white slave" trade. Also entering the battle were the American Society for Sanitary and Moral Prophylaxis (1905), the New York Social Hygiene Society (bankrolled by John D. Rockefeller Jr.'s millions), the Bureau of Social Hygiene (1911), and the American Social Hygiene Assocation. (1913).

Anthony Comstock, whose Society for Suppression of Vice
was a strident voice against immorality.
(Courtesy of Dictionary of American Portraits)

John D. Rockefeller, oil magnate and finacier
who bankrolled the New York Social Hygiene Society,
and helped establish the Eugenics Records Office.
(*Courtesy of Dictionary of American Portraits*)

3.

Heroin has been called a plague countless times. And the Dope Fiend has likewise been compared to — and then literalized as — a carrier of contagion. For instance, Dr. Burr in 1916 wrote that a "fruitful source of opium and morphine addiction is the presence of one mischievous person who is a confirmed habitué. I have known a whole neighborhood to be infected by a single individual of this character."[17] The following year, Dr. A. Gordon expanded on this notion: "Morphinomania is entered by the door of pain, of sexual passion, of sorrow, but also by the door of contagion."[18]

To fully grasp this pervasive belief, we need to have a clear sense of hygiene, germs and protoplasms as they were understood during the Golden Age of Purity. Hygiene has been variously defined as the science of living, and a system by which best health is maintained. In America, and to a lesser degree in Western Europe, what began as a system for promoting physical well-being became an all-encompassing vision laden with religious symbols and ideals. Not just good health but salvation could come to the righteous through sanitation. The helpful and harmful, the good and the bad were easily differentiated — no grays, only stark black and pure white.

In his remarkable book on the ritual persecution of drug users, *Ceremonial Chemistry*, Thomas Szasz explains clearly the underlying dynamic that must be kept in mind here:

> Any idea or act that gives men and women a sense
> of what their life is about or for — that, in other
> words, gives their existence meaning and purpose
> — is, properly speaking, religious. Science, medi-
> cine, and especially health and therapy are thus
> admirably suited to function as quasi-religious
> ideas, values and pursuits. It is necessary therefore,
> to distinguish between science as science, and sci-
> ence as religion (sometimes called "scientism").[19]

Hygiene, as a form of scientism, reached its ultimate
expression in the mania for eugenics that swept the U.S.
between the turn of the century and the beginning of
World War Two. At the root of this cultish craze was an
obsession with "protoplasm." Originally, this term meant
the formative material of young embryos. But by the
1890s it had been transformed into a crypto-religious essence: the basic substance of all living beings.

Ill-defined and ill-understood, "protoplasm" came to
have overtly spiritual meaning in the hands of hygienic
crusaders in the early 1900s. It was supposedly a secular,
scientific term, yet eugenicists repeated it like a holy
word. Charles Davenport, the most important eugenicist
in the U.S., used to "lift up his eyes reverently and with
his hands upraised as through in supplication, quiver
emotionally as he breathed 'protoplasm, we want more
protoplasm.'"[20]

What exactly these reformers and crusaders thought
protoplasm was is not clear. But we see here the dynamic
that will recur throughout the story of heroin's demonization: the physical becoming metaphorized, and then
the metaphor itself becoming literalized in order to create new "truth" or "knowledge." Faulty scientific understanding, religious belief and deep fears merged to create

a cultish world-view. Disbelievers (or outsiders) were suspect, if not instantly guilty. Those who dared to challenge the "obvious truth" of the matter were heretics. The word "inquisition" may be too strong, but there are many similarities between the cleansing of Europe of its heretics, witches and Jews, and the cleansing of the U.S. of its defective germ plasm.

The idea of contagion shifted in the 1880s and '90s. The work of Louis Pasteur, Robert Koch and Joseph Lister demonstrated an inarguable link between bacteria and disease. Evangelical proponents of hygiene embraced this new understanding, believing it to be scientific proof of their equation of moral and physical cleanliness. Though popular knowledge of germs lagged behind scientific research, slowly the germ theory replaced the older miasma theory (which argued that foul, nebulous vapors caused illness). Invisible enemies perceptible only by experts, germs to a certain degree reflect the age-old belief in demonic powers. Ritual cleansing, strenuous exorcisms — the diabolic spirit and the microbe had more similarities in the popular mind than we generally credit.

As the 20th century loomed closer, the words "pollution" and "purity" were heard more often from pulpits. And now they had the added weight of scientific proof. Religion bowed often now to science. Courtroom witnesses were no longer required to kiss the Bible, for fear of germs. And the common cup was replaced by more sanitary methods for participating in communion. In 1893, the first hygienic individual communion cup was introduced. Though there were pockets of resistance, the powers of scientific authority came to outweigh tradition. Germs were real, and the course of contagion was well understood; therefore, religion had to change. By 1905, most denominations had abandoned the millennia-long practice of the common chalice.

By the end of the 1880s — at least in the minds of public health officials — the old miasmic theory was discredited. Street cars, paper money, and library books were thought to harbor dangerous microbes. But no source of germs was so feared as the "unwashed" immigrants in the slums of the great cities. Known as "mudsills," immigrants from Southern and Eastern Europe were perceived as both physically and morally defiled. Much effort was placed on teaching them the "American Way" of hygiene. More frightening, more alien, more readily seen as agents of contamination, however, were the Chinese. And their role in the demonization of heroin and the creation of the Dope Fiend is crucial.

Dope

4.

As the ethnic makeup of the U.S. shifted, "native" citizens (meaning those whose ancestors came here before the Civil War) felt an increasing distrust, resentment and anxiety toward foreigners. According to America eugenicists, the 1870 and 1880 censuses proved that the immigrant population was growing much faster than the so-called native population. They feared that the WASP complexion of the U.S. was being steadily darkened by the higher birth rate of immigrants and blacks. Published in 1916 (and later, highly praised by Adolf Hitler) *The Passing of the Great Race* claimed that "higher orders of white races" interbreeding with Southern Europeans would result in "mongrelization."[21] Foreigners were, in short, a genetic threat. As though in a protoplasmic cold war, eugenic leaders lashed their followers into frenzies of fear with stories of "mongrel hordes of Southern Europe" and the Yellow Peril from Asia overwhelming the purity of American natives.

Charles Davenport saw little difference between national and ethnic identity. He claimed that Italians, Irish, Poles and "Hebrews" were all biologically distinct races. And he asserted that Jews were "intermediate between slovenly Servians and Greeks and the tidy Swedes, Germans and Bohemians." Italians were prone to crimes of violence, and Poles were self-reliant and clannish. Davenport, speaking as head of the highly influential Eugenic Records Office, railed against the influx of immigrants, who would make the population of the U.S. "darker in pigmentation, smaller in stature... more given to crimes of larceny, kidnapping, assault, murder, rape and sex-immorality."[22]

As a response to these "torrents of degenerate and defective protoplasm" sweeping over the nation, leaders of the "Eugenics cult," as Clarence Darrow described it, proposed and had enacted a series of laws to prevent "racial suicide" — reproduction by those of inferior genetic stock.

Eugenics claimed to be the science devoted to the improvement of the human race through the control of hereditary factors in mating. While this may seem simple and straightforward, as neutral as breeding a better milk cow, it was in fact only a small part of the story. Eugenics was a scientific craze, a pervasive philosophy, a cure-all for all societal ills, a system of interclass warfare and a new manifestation of the old Puritan hatred and fear of the human body. It first gained scientific acceptance, then popular support, and finally — making its way into the legal system — was enshrined as the new anti-sex gospel.

Indiana enacted the world's first sterilization statute in 1907. Soon, more than half of the United States had created laws inflicting sterilization on undesirables. These laws were aimed nominally at sex offenders and habitual criminals. And though some eugenicists believed that the laws had humanitarian underpinnings, their punitive nature can not be argued away. The sex organs, as the focus of the eugenicists' hate and fear, became the primary target. Castration was on occasion employed, though generally tubal ligation and vasectomy were prescribed.

The repressed content of these laws is obvious: the flesh was not the enemy in mere secular terms, but as religious dogma. The sexual human body was the prime battleground, the most tenacious stronghold of enemy resistance. The eugenics mania that swept the U.S. between 1880 and 1930 was the most violent manifestation of the body-dread that continues to haunt the American soul.

The word "eugenics" was first used 1883, by Francis Galton. He coined the term from Greek roots that mean "good birth" or "noble heredity." Though the word itself didn't appear in print until the 1880s, he'd preached eugenic theory well before then. In 1865, he authored an article in McMillan's Magazine in which he proposed that the state institute competitive examinations in hereditary merit. The winners would be celebrated in a mass wedding at Westminster Abbey and would be encouraged by grants from the state to produce many eugenically superior children. The unworthy, he suggested, should be segregated in convents and monasteries where they wouldn't be able to propagate their kind.[23]

As did almost all major figures in the eugenics movement, Galton grew up in a middle-class family plagued by extremes of religious feeling. He was prone to nervous disorders, and was frequently affected by dizziness, palpitations, wooziness and other signs of what would be called now a nervous breakdown. Though he was as an adult anti-religious, eugenics served as a substitute faith, a spiritual system that gave order and meaning to his world. It was, in short, "the religion of the future."[24]

Obsessed with counting, he spent a great deal of his time enumerating human characteristics. He became convinced that through selective breeding, the human race would be improved. As did many scientists of his day, he believed firmly in numerical objectivity, that observation and counting would give scientists a perfectly clear understanding of human nature. Tormented by doubt, nervous turmoil, and religious uncertainty, Galton embraced numerical certitude in hopes that perfection could be found within its sterile precincts.

Much impressed by his cousin's *Origin of Species*, Galton spoke of Darwinism as a therapy or medicine to cure the race of superstition and nightmare. Just as Darwinians saw evolution as a process by which "perfected" mankind had developed, so Galton believed that by winnowing out bad, or "cacogenic," strains of human germ plasm, humanity could reach a higher state. "What nature does blindly, slowly and ruthlessly, man may do providently, quickly and kindly."[25]

Another religion-haunted scientist, the man who carried the flame of eugenics to the new world and set the entire nation ablaze, was Charles Davenport. He, too, grew up in a hyper-Christian home, with an oppressive, Puritanical, hot-tempered father. He, too, rejected patriarchal piety, and replaced it with an obsessional religiosity of another kind: the worship of science, the crusade to improve humankind through eugenics.

In 1904, he persuaded the Carnegie Institution — one of the primary social-hygiene organizations of its day — to establish a station for experimental study of evolution. Under his directorship, it was set up at Cold Springs Harbor on Long Island, about 30 miles from New York. Five years later, he convinced one of his protégés, Mary Harriman, to approach her mother (widow of railroad tycoon E.H. Harriman) in hopes of gaining monetary support for further eugenic research. Mrs. Harriman was intrigued by Davenport's ideas, and funded the establishment of the Eugenics Records Office. With her money, 75 acres were purchased near Davenport's Cold Spring

Harbor station. Her money also went toward operating expenses and salaries for field workers, who numbered between 1911 and 1924 over 2,000. "What a fire you have kindled!" Davenport wrote to his benefactor soon after the Records Office was opened. "It is going to be a purifying *conflagration* some day!" (emphasis in the original.)[26]

Pleased with his work, Mrs. Harriman contributed steadily until 1918, when the entire installation was turned over to the Carnegie Institution. All told, her patronage came to over $500,000. Other millionaires, including John D. Rockefeller Jr. and George Eastman, contributed to the cause.

As was the case of Galton, the Eugenics Records Office and its many field workers were devoted to enumeration, compiling vast stores of data on the human gene pool. With little training, only a few weeks in some cases, the researchers would go out to compile as much information as they could on selected — usually rural — families. The cacogenic traits they looked for included obvious physical handicaps such as blindness and deafness. But in general the so-called dysgenic traits tended to be much more socially determined: sexual immorality, alcoholism, criminality, nomadism, shiftlessness, and even an excessive love of the sea. Retardation or "feeble-mindedness" was one of the characteristics that was thought particularly undesirable, yet how this was determined was vague at best. Many individuals were categorized as feeble-minded based purely on their poverty, refusal to work, or criminal record.

Clearly there was a bias to the eugenicsts' work. Any behavior that didn't mesh with the white upper middle class worldview was deemed dysgenic. Almost universally, eugenics workers and theorists were well-educated, Protestant and of Anglo-Saxon background. They tended to be from the professional classes: clerics, writers, professors. They were a public-minded group, abreast of science and contemptuous of superstition and old-fashioned ways. They were liberal and progressive, with a surprisingly high number of women in their ranks.

One holdover, however, from more tradition-bound times was the obsession with carnal purity. Davenport was appalled by even the suggestion of sexual self-indulgence. Virginal before his marriage, his Victorian-Puritanical childhood had been oppressive and pleasure-less. He was opposed to birth control largely because it encouraged, he claimed, sexual excess. He frequently placed sexual immorality in the same category as feeble-mindedness and propensities for crime. His hatred of the Jews was bolstered by the conviction that they exhibited the "greatest proportion of offenses against chastity and in connection with prostitution, the lowest of crimes."[27]

In his study of so-called wayward girls, he promoted the notion that the cause of prostitution was not poverty but "innate eroticism."[28] He was convinced that the brain contained a center for eroticism, similar to the speech center. In normal (meaning: white, upper-middle-class) people, the erotic center was controlled by a genetically determined governor. He coined the term "feebly inhibited" to describe these individuals whose governor was not strong enough to control their erotic urges.

Though he was in favor of segregation of the unfit to prevent procreation, he believed that castration, not vasectomy, should be used on the cacogenic males. Vasectomy prevented fertility, but not desire, and separating the sex act from its procreative consequences would be an encouragement to rapists. Also, castration "cuts off the hormones and makes the patient docile, tractable, and without sex desire."[29] In other words, a perfect citizen.

Eugenics, by its nature, was about sex. And eugenicists spent a great deal of their time and effort on the question of other peoples' sex lives, especially those of the so-called feeble-minded. While there was some disagreement whether feeble-minded men were over- or under-sexed, there was unanimity regarding women: they were unalterably over-sexed, uncontrollable and unashamed. Given that a weaker intellect accompanied a weaker sense of inhibition, it followed that retarded women were much more lustful than normal women. Eugenicists displayed a remarkable adeptness with circular reasoning: sexual immorality was a sign of feeble-mindedness and feeble-mindedness was compelling proof of sexual immorality.

The two most famous victims of American eugenics were both young, sexually attractive women trapped in institutions. Deborah Kallikak (a fictitious name: Kalla from the Greek word for good, and Kak for bad) was institutionalized for 81 years, the daughter of a poor woman who sent her to the Vineland Training School in New Jersey after marrying a man who wasn't Deborah's father. The study based on Deborah's family history, *The Kallikak Family: a Study in the Heredity of Feeble-mindedness*, shaped much of eugenic thought. It purported to trace the lineage of two sides of Deborah's family: one with pure Quaker blood and one tainted by "bad seed." Though she was classified as feeble-mined, evidence of her abilities (music, crafts, wood-working) were obvious. Her charm and beauty were unquestioned.

Eugene Doll, an administrator at the Vineland School, said, "hers was a body which moved with the full knowledge of the impact its movements had on the opposite sex."[30] Based on such "evidence" she was deemed sexually immoral. The combination of indigence, helplessness and attractiveness made her a likely candidate for eugenic interference.

Another case, that of Carrie Buck, put the stamp of legitimacy on the eugenics laws. Young and pregnant, classified as a "moral imbecile," she was scheduled for sterilization to prevent her "tainted spoor" from being passed on to another generation. A legal battle ensued, and in 1927 the case reached the U.S. Supreme Court, which declared the law constitutional. Oliver Wendell Holmes Jr. wrote the majority opinion on the Buck case, declaring that "three generations of imbeciles are enough."

Besides the Kallikak book, dozens of other family studies were produced between 1877 and 1926. Often bankrolled by the Eugenics Records Office, these studies set out to prove the hereditary nature of feeblemindedness by studying human pedigrees. Giving the families bizarre pseudonyms (the Nams, Jukes, Daks, etc.), fudging facts, and even altering photos to make the subjects seem more alien, these studies make more sense as fiction than as science. The Pineys of New Jersey were another group who were studied in order to be controlled. Elizabeth Kite, one of the Vineland field workers, wrote a fanciful, factually inhibited book which includes this explanation of the Pineys' nature:

> Like the degenerate relative of the crab that ages ago gave up a free roving life, and gluing its head to a rock, built a wall of defense around itself,

spending the rest of its life kicking food into its mouth and enjoying the functionings of reproduction, the Piney and all the rest of his type have become barnacles upon our civilization, all the higher functions of whose manhood have been atrophied through disuse.[31]

Other studies used pseudo-science, cooked statistics and pure invention to paint a picture of American culture riddled with pockets of "degenerate protoplasm," festering sores ready to burst and spill their infectious essences on the hygienic white culture. Many of the studies became popular reading material, and the Kallikak book was seriously considered for Broadway.

Like all science, eugenic research was heavily colored by the social and moral structure from which it grew. But in the case of eugenics, the belief systems are more overt and unmistakable than is usual.

Plainly put, eugenics was a religion. Shaped almost entirely by people who'd lost their faith in traditional religion, eugenics was nonetheless referred to as "gospel," and scientists as the "new priesthood." Galton expected that eugenics would provide a secular alternative to religion, yet his — like most others' — view was still profoundly religious. Original sin was reconfigured as genetic taint. Moral elevation was the goal: eugenicists talked of supermen and fitter families as a minister might talk of saints and the elect. The American Eugenics Society even launched a eugenics sermon contest to bring together the genetic gospel and organized Christianity.

Albert Wiggam, a journalist, author and lecturer, wrote a 1923 bestseller called *The New Decalogue of Science*, in which he claimed that eugenics was "simply the projection of the Golden Rule down the stream of protoplasm."

His motto was "Do unto the unborn as you would have
the born and unborn do to you." For Wiggam, religion
and science were inextricable;

> In our day, instead of using tables of stone, burning
> bushes, prophesies and dreams to reveal God's will,
> he has given men the microscope, the spectroscope,
> the telescope, the chemist's test tube and the stat-
> istician's curve in order to enable men to make
> their own revelations. These instruments of divine
> revelation have not only added an enormous range
> of new commandments — an entirely new De-
> calogue to man's moral codes, but they have sup-
> plied him with the technique for putting the old
> ones into effect.[32]

A *Eugenics Catechism* was published by the American
Eugenics Society in 1926. It includes questions and an-
swers á la a Catholic catechism, merging Biblical and scientific faith:

> "Q: what is the most precious thing in the world?
> A: The human gene plasm."[33]

If eugenics was kind of faith, then it, like all other organized religions, was more about social control than
true spirituality. Those who gained the most from the
triumph of eugenics were the professionals — institutional staff, mental health workers, welfare bureaucrats,
prison officials — who were in the business of shaping
social structure and maintaining the status quo.

By the eve of World War Two, at least 27,000 compulsory sterilizations had taken place in the U.S.[34] It took the
rise of the Third Reich, which pushed eugenics to its

logical conclusion, to disabuse Americans of their infatuation with eugenics. The most zealous of compulsory sterilization advocates was Harry Laughlin, brought to the E.R.O. in 1917 by Davenport. Laughlin was instrumental in the enactment of state sterilization laws, and developed model legislation which he presented to states as well as foreign governments. The Virginia statute declared constitutional in 1927 was based on Laughlin's work.

Six years later, Nazi Germany enacted its first Hereditary Health Law. As in the American plan, the law was designed to ensure that racially unworthy individuals not pass on their "bad seed." In *The Nazi Connection,* Stefan Kühl examines the direct links between American racist eugenics and Nazi racial policy. He presents new evidence that the entire debate about mass sterilization in Germany was deeply influenced by America's groundbreaking work in the field. Books such as *The Rising Tide of Color Against White-World-Supremacy* and *The Revolt Against Civilization* were much read and taken very seriously in Germany as well as the U.S.

Adolf Hitler himself was affected by American eugenic thought. In *Mein Kampf* he records his admiration for the American Immigration Act of 1924. Otto Wagener, a ranking Nazi, quoted Hitler as telling him, "I have studied with great interest the laws of several American states concerning the prevention of reproduction by people whose progeny would, in all probability, be of no value or be injurious to the racial stock."[35] Hitler was so impressed with Madison Grant's *The Passing of the Great Race* that he sent him a letter of gratitude, telling Grant that the book was "his Bible."[36] Leon Whitney, author of

The Case for Sterilization, also received written congratulations from the Führer.

From Hitler on down, Nazi thought regarding "racial undesirables" was heavily affected by eugenics laws in the U.S.:

> American eugenicists were conscious and proud of their impact on legislation in Nazi Germany. They recognized that the German Law on Preventing Hereditarily Ill Progeny was influenced by the California sterilization law and designed after the Model Eugenic Sterilization Law, developed by Harry Laughlin in 1922. The German law followed Laughlin's in terms of basic guidelines, but was slightly more moderate.[37]

The German law was implemented with great enthusiasm and speed. Heredity courts were established, comprising of two doctors and a judge appointed by the state. After one year, more than 56,000 people had been deemed defective and were sterilized.[38] Hitler's diligence and devotion were praised by American eugenicsts; German academics likewise applauded their American counterparts. In 1936, the University of Heidelberg bestowed an honorary doctorate on Harry Laughlin, by then in charge of Eugenics Records Office and still an enthusiastic supporter of sterilization. In accepting the award, Laughlin said, "To me this honor will be doubly valued because it will come from a nation which for many centuries nurtured the human seed-stock which later founded my country and thus gave basic character to our present lives and institutions."[39]

The year before, the German government had instituted the Nuremberg Laws, an extension of the eugenics statutes already on the books. These Racial Hygiene Laws banned marriage between Jews and non-Jews as a method of "purifying" the German gene-pool. Though at this stage, the German sterilization program was not connected directly with hatred of the Jews, as Hitler's rage and fear were progressively manifested into law, the racial and eugenic programs were merged. The line between racially inferior and genetically tainted rapidly blurred. The blind, retarded, deaf, schizophrenic, epileptic, manic-depressive and even alcoholic were all slated for sterilization. Estimates vary, but it is reasonable to assume that more than 20,000,000 people were found defective and sterilized between 1933 and 1945.[40]

And of course it's no great leap from eugenic sterilization to racial extermination. The hatred for Jews, blacks, Chinese, and other racially unacceptable groups in the U.S. was reflected, amplified, and acted on in the death camps of Nazi Germany. Just as sterilization programs became euthanasia programs — killing first the mentally ill and retarded inmates of institutions, then physically handicapped children and adults — so it was simple for the Germans to expand their racial hygiene efforts from merely prohibiting the conception and birth of racially inferior children to the killing of those who were thought to be a moral, social or biological threat to the state.

The Nazi ideology of purity depended heavily on the use of disease and contagion metaphors. Nazis declared that those of mixed "racial" origin were like syphilis, infecting the German gene pool. The so-called Jewish problem was repeatedly compared to syphilis, and to cancer that must be cut out for the sanctity of the German protoplasm. As early as 1919, in Hitler's first published tract, he accused Judaism of carrying a "racial tuberculosis among the nations."[41] Across the Atlantic, at the same time, American social scientists, lawmakers and moral crusaders were using strikingly similar analogies to demonize their own "dysgenic" populations.

5.

What exactly is "purity?" Numerous thinkers have attempted to untangle this knotty question, which is, I believe, at the heart of the Dope Fiend mythos. Various explanations are available; almost all are — on a deep level — built on the notion of boundaries and boundary violation. Dirt, disorder, disease, danger: all of these have at their root the idea of the border which must not be crossed.

A useful place to begin is with Mikhail Bakhtin's theory of the grotesque body. In his work on Rabelais, the Soviet critic analyzes a shift from what he calls the grotesque sphere of life to the New Bodily Canon. The essence of the grotesque of Bakhtin is that it is not impenetrable, but open, "a body in the act of becoming. It is never finished, never completed; it is continuously built, created, and builds and creates another body."[42]

In the New Bodily Canon, which evolved alongside Western industrialization, the human form is entirely finished, strictly limited. All orifices of this form are sealed shut. This new ideology of the flesh presents an impervious facade, a closed realm, machine-like in its rigidity, sterile and hard as surgical steel. The grotesque body not only stands in opposition to this closed, finished, impenetrable form, but also refutes and mocks it.

"The three main acts in life of the grotesque body are sexual intercourse, death throes, and the act of birth. Frequently these three acts are transformed or merged into each other."[43] Boundaries blur; life seen this way is a constantly evolving, constantly interpenetrating system. The sex organs, the excretory organs, the nipples and mouth and nose: all of these have in common the function of allowing interpenetration between bodies and exchange between bodies and the world. As we eat and breathe, the world enters each of us, is stripped for useful parts, and then expelled. It's no coincidence, then, that most rules regarding ritual purity are concerned with the basic biological functions. For it's here that our interconnectedness is most obvious, our fundamental incompleteness is seen.

In the vastness of the grotesque, according to Bakhtin, the official European bodily canon is but a tiny island, though we who live on it perceive it as a huge continent. For only a few hundred years, and only in certain official literatures, sciences, arts and social systems, has the sealed and impenetrable body been the norm. Bakhtin refers to the "boundless ocean of imagery" that manifests and celebrates the grotesque body. All ancient societies and languages, and almost all non-Western cultures, have at their heart a fundamental grotesqueness. In opposition to this — in Europe and America — a rigid, aggressively dualistic, combative world-view developed. The boundaries, the borders, between categories must be protected at all costs.

Peter Lamborn Wilson develops this analysis further, arguing that the paranoia and free-floating anxieties which manifest in hysterical campaigns for "safety" and "purity" are based on a dread of the basic amorphousness of life. The "placental wetness of becoming" is not a threat to life, but essential to it, no matter how much crusaders for purity howl against it. "Juice and slime are the ultimate free-form connective and penetrative tissues of living systems. Life clearly has no interest in the antibiotic hermeticism implied in such phrases as 'boundary violation.'"[44] Fighting against the grotesque, against life itself, perhaps, is the New Bodily Canon, which currently takes the form of crusades against impurity, wars against drugs and poverty, and increasingly aggressive surveillance. Polluting forces must be located quickly, targeted, and thoroughly eradicated.

"Protectionism becomes the one true philosophy of any culture based on mass anxiety about border violations; 'safety' and 'survival' its shibboleths and highest values. The 'security state' emerged like an abstract constellation figured against a random patterning of stars — each representing a threatened job (immigrant invasion), dysfunctional family (the implosion of the middle-class ideal), crime-ridden neighborhood (dope fiends descending on pure American space), the black hole of boredom ('idle hands are the devil's workshop')."[45]

Another way of understanding pollution is the notion of dirt as the essence or inescapable proof of death. As Lawrence Distasi says, "if there is anything that typifies modern culture, it is certainly alienation from the ground which it flies over and rolls over and chemicalizes over and paves over in its vain attempt not to touch it, not to die."[46]

Terence McLaughlin, in *Dirt: a Social History*, addresses the question from a slightly different angle, but still the basic understanding is the same. "Dirt is evidence of the imperfections of life, a constant reminder of change and decay. It is the dark side of all human activities — human, because it's only in our judgment that things are dirty; there is no such thing as absolute dirt."[46] He bases his argument partially on a discussion of contamination in *Being and Nothingness*, where Sartre concerns himself — one might say is obsessed with — "slime." It attaches itself to us and will not let go. "It is soft yielding action, moist and feminine sucking, it lives obscurely under my fingers."[47] But doubly troubling, it also acts as a solvent: breaking down the boundary of the skin. We hate slime because we fear becoming slime. "We are jealous of our 'oneness,' our individuality, and we resent and fear any situation that forces us to become intimate, in the real sense of the word, with another person against our will."[48]

Mary Douglas would agree with McLaughlin that dirt is "matter out of place." In *Purity and Danger* she analyzes the cultural connections between dirt and chaos, and argues that rituals of purification have been developed to control this perceived threat. Hygiene and its opposite — filth — represent two primary states of being: order and chaos. All thresholds (whether orifices, wounds, or other unnatural penetrations) are a serious threat to the stability of the structure. We might call these places chaos-incursion zones, the points where ordinary duelist categories (either/or) do not function. The refusal of anything to fit neatly into a category (i.e., interior/exterior, hidden/revealed, contaminating/therapeutic) creates a state of anxiety and danger to the integrity of the actual body and body-as-culture.

If, as Douglas argues, the human body stands as a potent symbol of human culture, and if the thresholds of the body represent areas of power and danger, then we should expect instances of bodily penetration to be especially laden with significance.

And no instrument, no tool or weapon, has the symbolic contaminating power of the hypodermic needle. In the hands of the Dope Fiend, it took on the role of both threat to individual well-being and to the sanctity and stability of American culture. In short, it became the ultimate agent of violation.

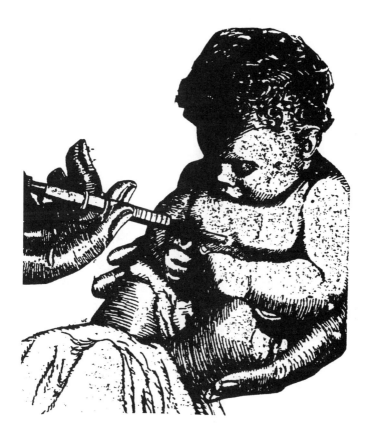

6.

In Dope Fiend iconography, in the paranoid fantasies and hysterical calls-to-arms which were crucial to the demonization of heroin, the hypodermic needle stands as the most potent symbol of moral and physical transgression. In the first two decades of the 20th century, when users of opiates were transfigured into the ultimate threat to American purity, the syringe appeared increasingly in editorial cartoons and newspaper illustrations as a kind of satanic stinger. With a wicked point at one end and a load of lethal venom at the other, it became the perfect emblem of contamination. Like a perversely mechanized phallus (the essence of rape manifested in high-tech steel), heavy with toxic slime, hard and sharp enough to penetrate any skin boundary, the hypodermic was a fitting addition to the iconography of the Dope Fiend. The pirate his cutlass, the gangster his tommy-gun, the scalp-mad Indian his tomahawk, the anarchist his hissing black-sphere bomb — and the Dope Fiend, his hypo.

Hypodermic Needle — the utlimate tool of defilement.

Compared to other items in the doctor's armamentarium, the hypodermic syringe was a relatively late addition. Physicians had given opiates mostly by mouth, but they'd also tried dusting the powder into wounds, through massage, in blisters and enemas. Use of the lancet came next: incising the skin and pouring in the drug. In the mid-1600s, Sir Christopher Wren proposed a method of cutting the patient's skin and attaching quills through which medicine might be infused into the blood stream. Drs. Boyle and Wilkins experimented with this method, drugging dogs with opium.

Though there is some dispute, Alexander Wood of Edinburgh is generally credited with the development of hypodermic injection. His needle, however, had no point, and no lateral openings for the medication to escape through. In his method, at least early on, it was necessary to cut the skin before pressing in the syringe. The honor that goes inarguably to Dr. Wood is for creating the first needle habitué — his wife. A user of injected morphine, Mrs. Wood died of an overdose, likely at her husband's hands.[50]

Who was the first is less important than the trend toward general use of the new tool. In the late 1850s, hardly any doctor had heard of intravenous injection. By the late 1870s, the syringe was standard issue in the doctor's black bag. It wasn't long before the instrument acquired significance far beyond its therapeutic uses. Comparisons were made to sabre and pistol — doctors standing ready to charge into battle against disease. Perhaps the military metaphors were influenced by the American Civil War — often credited with popularizing the needle. The first American textbook on hypodermic injection was published in 1865, and in the following three decades the needle was seen, increasingly, as a powerful symbol of progress, with medicine and technology forging a close alliance.

A few voices warned against the indiscriminate use of the needle. Nonetheless, it became *the* symbol of medical triumph in the late 1800s. "The medical journals of the day were full of enthusiastic descriptions of new successes in therapeutics through the hypodermic use of morphine and it is very doubtful if any painful condition to which the human race is heir escaped the list of those for which the drug was recommended."[50] Achieving nearly omnipresent status, the hypodermic was offered by such an archetypically American source as the Sears and Roebuck catalog. The year before heroin was released, the catalog offered a standard syringe kit for $1.50 and a deluxe model of $2.75.[51]

It reached well beyond the world of healing, however. "Now that the hypodermic use of morphia is brought into sensational novels as a melodramatic device, it may indeed be said to have reached the height of fashion," Dr. Allbut complained in 1870.[52] The needle even became faddish as jewelry: a stylish object which society women wore as fobs, pendants and charms. Dr. Pichon noted in 1889 that "...the expensive and artistic syringes and solution containers that are for sale are evidently not manufactured for medical or therapeutic purposes."[53]

The hypodermic was responsible for an important change in the notion of morphine abuse. As long as the opiates were taken orally, the term "appetite" seemed appropriate to described the desire for the drug. With the popularity of the needle, "appetite" was less commonly used — supplanted by "habit" and "mania." Also, moving the point of entry away from the mouth contributed to the disconnection of opiates and alcohol (with which it had long been associated).

Injecting morphine and heroin gave users a more potent effect. Smaller and more accurately measured doses were also easier with the hypodermic. But it appears that most significant was the penetrative nature of the needle. If the body is the society in miniature, then a device that readily penetrates the boundaries, makes a mockery of the skin border, and can easily drive a potent intoxicating substance deep into the recesses of the body is an excellent symbol for impurity and pollution on the cultural level.

In the following chapter, discussing in depth the course of heroin's demonization, we'll see the needle used repeatedly as an emblem of violation. Like heroin — praised as a panacea at first — so too the hypodermic needle could not become so thoroughly hated and feared if it had not been first so trusted and beloved. And, like heroin, it was used symbolically again and again, as a weapon in the covert wars of purification that raged throughout America in the early 20th century.

Notes:

1. Van de Warker, Ely. "The Fetish [sic] of the Ovary." *American Journal of Obstetrics.* (54) July-December 1906. p.371.
2. Mather, Cotton. *Magnalia Christi Americana.* (London) 1702. Book VII, Chapter 1, par. 1.
3. Mather, Cotton. *Magnalia Christi Americana.* (London) 1702. Book 1, Chapter 2.

4. Duffy, John. *The Healers.* (New York: McGraw Hill) 1976. p. 29.
5. Beall, Otho. "Cotton Mather: The First Significant Figure in American Medicine." in: *Bulletin of the History of Medicine.* March-April 1952. p. 103.
6. Hoy, Suellen. *Chasing Dirt: the American Pursuit of Cleanliness.* (New York: Oxford U.P.) 1995. p. 3.
7. Franklin, Benjamin. *The Autobiography of Benjamin Franklin.* (New Haven: Yale U.P.) 1964. pp. 149-150.
8. Sweet, Leonard. *Health and Medicine in the Evangelical Tradition.* (Valley Forge, PA: Trinity) 1994. p. 117.
9. *Ibid.,* p. 117.
10. Bushman, Richard and Claudia Bushman. "The Early History of Cleanliness in America." in: *Journal of American History.* March 1988. p. 1218.
11. Rosenberg, Charles and Carroll Smith-Roseberg. "Pietism and the Origins of the American Public Health Movement." in: *Sickness and Health in America.* Ed: Leavitt and Numbers. p. 388.
12. Furnas, Joseph. *The Life and Times of the Late Demon Rum.* (New York: Putnams) 1965. p. 219.
13. *Ibid.,* p. 220.
14. *Poems Teachers Ask For.* (Dansville, NY: F.A. Owens Co.) p. 79.
15. Sweet, Leonard. *Health and Medicine in the Evangelical Tradition.* (Valley Forge, PA: Trinity) 1994. p. 119.
16. Nation, Carry A. *The Use and Need of the Life of Carry A. Nation.* (Topeka: F.M. Steves) 1909. p. 130.
17. Terry, Charles and Mildred Pellens. *The Opium Problem.* (New York, Committee on Drug Addictions). 1928. p. 116.

18. *Ibid.*, p. 151.
19. Szasz, Thomas. *Ceremonial Chemistry.* (New York: Doubleday). 1974. p. 3.
20. Kevles, Daniel. *In the Name of Eugenics.* (New York: Knopf). 1985. p. 52.
21. Kühl, Stefan. *The Nazi Connection.* (New York: Oxford U.P.). 1994. p. 85.
22. Davenport, Charles. *Heredity in Relation to Eugenics.* (New York: Henry Holt). 1911. pp. 216, 218-219, 221-222.
23. Galton, Francis. "Hereditary Talent and Character." *McMillans Magazine.* (12) 1865. pp. 157-166, 318-327.
24. Kühl, Stefan. *The Nazi Connection.* (New York: Oxford U.P.). 1994. p. 16.
25. Galton, Francis. *Essays in Eugenics.* (Eugenics Education Society) 1909. p. 42.
26. Davenport, Charles, to Mrs. E. Harriman, February 21, 1911. In C. Davenport Papers, Harriman file.
27. Kevles, Daniel. *In the Name of Eugenics.* (New York: Knopf). 1985. p. 53.
28. Davenport, Charles. *Heredity in Relation to Eugenics.* (New York: Henry Holt). 1911. p. 258.
29. Smith, J. David. *Minds Made Feeble.* (Rockville, Maryland: Aspen) 1985. p. 31.
30. *Ibid.*, p. 31.
31. Kite, Elizabeth. "The Pineys." *Survey.* October 4, 1913. p. xx.
32. Wiggam, Albert E. *The New Decalogue of Science.* (Bobbs-Merrill). 1923. p. 109.
33. *Eugenics Catechism*, 10.
34. Smith, J. David. *Minds Made Feeble.* (Rockville, Maryland: Aspen) 1985. p. 139.

35. Wagener, Otto. *Hitler Aus Nächster Nähe*. Ed: Henry Turner. (Frankfort: Ullstein) 1978. p. 264.
36. Kühl, Stefan. *The Nazi Connection*. (New York: Oxford U.P.). 1994. p. 85.
37. *Ibid.*, p. 39.
38. Smith, J. David. *Minds Made Feeble*. (Rockville, Maryland: Aspen) 1985. p. 156.
39. Laughlin, H.H. *Laughlin Notebooks: Vol. II, Nazi Eugenics*. (St. Louis, Missouri: Washington U.P.) n.p.
40. Smith, J. David. *Minds Made Feeble*. (Rockville, Maryland: Aspen) 1985. p. 156.
41. Sonntag, Susan. *Illness as Metaphor*. (New York: Farrar, Straus). 1977. pp. 83, 84.
42. Bakhtin, *Mikhail M. Rabelais and His World*. (Cambridge, Massachusetts: MIT Press) 1968. p. 317.
43. *Ibid.*, pp. 353-354.
44. Wilson, Peter L. "Boundary Violations." *Found Object*. Spring 1995. (5) 20-28. p. 26.
45. *Ibid.*, p. 24.
46. Distasi, Lawrence. *Mal Occhio*. (San Francisco: North Point Press) 1981. p. 141.
47. McLaughlin, Terence. *Dirt: a Social History*. (New York: Dorset). 1971. p. 1.
48. *Ibid.*, p. 3.
49. *Ibid.*, p. 3.
50. Krivanek, Jara. *Heroin*. (Sydney: Allen and Unwin). 1988. p. 32.
51. Terry, Charles and Mildred Pellens. *The Opium Problem*. (New York, Committee on Drug Addictions). 1928. p. 69.
52. Kandall, Stephen. *Substance and Shadow*. (Harvard U.P.) 1996. p. 22.

53. Terry, Charles and Mildred Pellens. *The Opium Problem.* (New York, Committee on Drug Addictions). 1928. p. 67.
54. *Ibid.,* p. 102.

Chapter Five
Descent Into Hell

1.

The Dope Fiend is an amalgam of many elements from American culture of the early 20th century. But no force was so crucial to its final form as the so-called Yellow Peril. This national convulsion is one of the best-known and obvious examples of racist hysteria in American history, as the population of an entire continent was cast as barely human, alien, threatening, tainted: a kind of racial contagion. As archetypal invading Others, Asians, especially Chinese, were resisted, feared, and maligned with a virulence that echoes to the present time.

It would appear that Americans have always had a deep need for racial enemies: an Other to project fear, suspicion, hate and envy onto, a quasi-human scapegoat figure against whom Americans define themselves. To be an "us," there has to be an inferior "them." It's almost as though this culture has a profound uncertainty of what it is, so the need for an image of what it isn't becomes overwhelmingly important.

Réne Girard, in his discussion of the sacrificial victim, argues that all cultures select the scapegoat from outside. "Between the victims and the community a crucial social link is missing."[1] Perhaps the victim is not literally from the outside, but some characteristics — racial, ethnic, sex, social class, religion — set the victim apart from the dominant culture. What's necessary for this process to function is that the victim is on some level *not human* in the same way that the sacrificers are. The conquerors of the New World certainly struggled with the question of the natives' humanness; the Roman Catholic Church was forced into the debate, deciding whether the Indians even had souls. The enslavement of thousands of Africans was also facilitated by this same notion. If an African and a European were human in the same way, then certain moral impediments would stand in the way of wholesale cultural annihilation. More recently, Nazi propagandists depicted their cultural enemies as vermin: rats, snakes, insects, carrion birds. Jews were not human in Nazi ideology in the same way that so-called Aryans were, thus making their enslavement and eventual destruction a matter of interspecies, not intercultural, conflict.

2.

In the U.S., it was common to treat Asians as fundamentally different than those of European "blood" or "germ plasm." Well before substantial Asian immigration into the U.S., traders and (more often) missionaries promoted extreme misrepresentations of the Chinese in their homeland. In the early 1800s, Protestant missionaries — partly as a way of drumming up more financial support for their efforts, and partly as a result of simple racism — described the Chinese as deep in the thrall of Satan. In particular, sexual perversion and excesses filled the pages of their reports. Fevered accounts of "orgies of idolatry" in which pagan rites were thinly disguised sexual frenzies, the participants exhibiting a "diabolical ecstasy," were common.[2] Heathen religion and sexual debauchery were indistinguishable for the missionaries: "Girls scarcely twelve years old were given up to the beastly passions of men. Parents prostituted their daughters; husbands their wives; brothers their sisters — and this they did with a diabolical joy."[3] Terms such as "vile," "polluted," and "debased" abound. Young white girls were never safe when in Chinese society, which might lure them with "pictures, songs and aphrodisiacs" into "the Gates of Hell to perform abominable acts."[4] The use of demonic imagery is not incidental; it is one of the characteristics of the American scapegoating process. Like the Puritan spiritual warriors in New England, missionaries to China saw themselves fighting a nearly omnipotent foe, a universal polluting essence. "Its corrupting and debasing influences pervade all classes of society. Forms of vice which in other lands sulk in dark

places, or appear only in the midnight orgies of the bac-
chanalian revelers, in China blanch not in the light of
noonday."[5] One editor reported that the Chinese butch-
ered young girls in order to "drink certain fluids from
their bodies." Also, "grains of rice steeped in freshly cut
gall bladder" were used for "magical, medicinal purposes."[6] Echoing the archetypal European slur on Judaism — that Christian children were captured and tor-
tured in "Jewish-Satanic" rites — a report in the *North
China Daily News* alleged that Christian children were
being kidnapped in Shanghai, and their eyes and "private
parts" were being sliced out to make "mysterious drugs."

Much of this lurid rhetoric reappeared in almost identical form once the Chinese began to emigrate to the U.S.
But in addition, a new layer of anxiety appeared: the fear
and resentment that Chinese workers were a threat to
"native" American laborers' livelihoods.

As the Chinese began entering the U.S. in the 1850s,
they had a major impact on the American labor market,
especially on the West Coast. In various jobs requiring
long hours of heavy toil — laundry, mining, farm work,
railroad construction — they succeeded, and often surpassed white workers. Putting in longer and more pro-
ductive hours, Chinese laborers were soon perceived as a
serious threat. And opium — which many Chinese workers smoked, and which contributed to their greater
stamina and tolerance for grueling labor — was painted
in the popular press as a menace to "American manhood." It's important to note that by most objective accounts, the Chinese in America were and continue to be
a far more law-abiding group than most others. Actual
arrests for robbery, rape, murder, etc. were consistently
lower than for the general population, even with the

slanders and hysteria influencing the police and courts. Still, because American labor unions felt deeply threatened by Chinese efficiency and hard work, they began a campaign to halt further immigration and to marginalize the roughly 100,000 Chinese who were in the U.S. by the time the Exclusion Act was passed by Congress in 1889. Led by its president, Samuel Gompers, the AFL carried out a decades-long vilification campaign against the Chinese. In 1902, Gompers co-authored a booklet called *Some Reasons for Chinese Exclusion: Meat Versus Rice; American Manhood Against Asiatic Coolieism — Which Shall Survive?* In this work, he argued that "The racial differences between American whites and Asiatics would never be overcome. The superior whites had to exclude the inferior Asiatics by law, or if necessary, by force of arms. The Yellow Man found it natural to lie, cheat, and murder and 99 out of 100 Chinese are gamblers."[7] By 1906, Gompers' rhetoric contained all the elements of American fear and hatred that drove eugenicists and later exploiters of drug-hysteria. "Maintenance of the nation depended on racial purity," he declared.[8] And regarding the archetypal den of drug iniquity, he wrote: "What other crimes were committed in those dark fetid places when those innocent victims of the Chinaman's viles [sic] were under the influence of the drug, are almost too horrible to imagine. There are hundreds, aye, thousands, of our American girls and boys who have acquired this deathly habit and are doomed, hopelessly doomed, beyond the shadow of redemption."[9] Though originating in crass economic motives, Gompers' seething fears took on a clearly religious tone. This was not just a struggle for jobs, but a war for the American soul.

Samuel Gompers, who led the American Federation of Labor's
campaign of defamement and malignment against the Chinese.
(Courtesy of Dictionary of American Portraits)

Responding to such battle cries, Congress banned the
importation of opium by Chinese, though allowing
Americans this right for another 20 years. In 1890, another law prohibited Chinese from processing smoking
opium, but continued to allow "native" entrepreneurs
this right until 1909, when opium smoking was banned
altogether. Why such a discrepancy? More than one
scholar[10] has argued that opium was seen as a "secret
weapon," a tool that gave the Chinese greater ability and
stamina, affording them an "unfair advantage" over
American workers.

Early 20th century depiction of a Chinese opium den.

3.

The Yellow Peril took a number of forms. For the purpose of better understanding the development of the Dope Fiend, four areas will be my focus: disease, race-mixing and sexual threat, slavery, and opium use.

The Yellow Peril soon became a familiar threat.

The Chinese — both in Asia and the U.S. — were associated with filth and diseases on countless occasions. And both of these concepts were crucial to the belief that Asians were a threat to America protoplasmic purity. In numerous reports during the Exclusion Act debates, medical metaphors were used — some so sloppily that it's impossible to tell whether the writers were referring to social, moral or physical pestilence. As the germ theory became known to the average American, it came to dominate thinking about the Chinese, whose settlements were referred to as "huge festering ulcers," nests, hives, dens, and cancers. And the "infectious diseases that germinate in the filth of that malodorous quarter" were feared to be spreading to nearby native communities.[11] Leprosy was a favorite disease with which to compare Chinese culture: "the Mongolian Blight."

From medieval anti-Jewish propaganda to the first vampire film, *Nosferatu*; from Old Testament ritual surrounding the spread of pestilence to the paranoia and hate-mongering that accompanied the early days of AIDS, plagues are frequently blamed on a foreign, "unnatural," presence. The Chinese menace was similarly explained in Dr. Arthur Stout's *Chinese Immigration and the Physiological Cause of Decay of a Nation*. This 1862 report conflates racial-mixture fears, crackpot medical theories and sheer nonsense.

According to Stout, "hereditary diseases" such as consumption, scrofula, syphilis and insanity were rife among the Chinese, and their foul habit of smoking opium contributed to the problem. Allowing the Chinese (and blacks, too) to stay in America would be like permitting "cancer" to eat away at the body politic. The "Divine Excellence" of the Anglo-Saxon race must not be polluted by "Asiatic horrors," Stout declared. "Until Islamism and Paganism alike sink into oblivion, and Christianity enters, like sunlight unto chaos, to illuminate and revivify this ancient world... we cannot permit Asiatics to enter."[12] Stout was not a lone voice crying in the wilderness. The A.M.A.'s evaluation of this report was in full agreement. "The evils likely to result from the combined intermixture of races and introduction of habits and customs of a sensual and depraved people in our midst, with hereditary vices and engrafted peculiarities" were more than sufficient cause to keep all aliens out.[13] Nine years later,

Dr. Stout sounded the warning cry again, in even more clamorous terms:

> Better it would be for our country that the hordes of Genghis Khan should overflow the land and with armed hostility devastate our valleys with sabre and the firebrand that these more pernicious hosts in the garb of friends should insidiously poison the well springs of life, and spreading far and wide, gradually undermine and corrode the vitals of our strength and prosperity.[14]

Besides leprosy and cancer, syphilis was a disease commonly blamed on Chinese contamination. More potent, more virulent than ordinary syphilis was the Chinese Pox or "Canton Ulcer." This "foul contagion," explained the editor of *The Medico Literary Journal* in 1878, "is progressively tainting the Anglo-Saxon blood."[15] J. Marion Sims — president of the A.M.A. and world-renowned for his gynecological experiments — asserted that every Chinese slave-prostitute "breeds moral and physical pestilence." On the West Coast, "even boys eight and ten years old have been syphilized by these degraded wretches."[16] The implication here, that the literal and metaphorical bloodstream was being poisoned, is obvious. So-called Chinese Afflictions were thought to be the result of a millennia-long history of "beastly vices, resistant to all the efforts of modern medicine."[17]

Fear of sexual disease is often, on a deep level, really a fear of genetic corruption. Sims' obsession with women's genital organs and the "seed" of young boys reflects a profound anxiety regarding America's reproductive abilities. These same fears surfaced again in the literature of "addiction;" many doctors fretted about opiates ruining the reproductive organs. "Generative functions are depressed by opium, and in chronic poisoning the menses cease and men become impotent. Passower has demonstrated that the abuse of morphine may occasion atrophy of the female organs."[18]

American children were particularly at risk from the "scourge of the hordes of China." Chinese servants were introducing their "loathsome diseases" and "debasing habits" into American homes. Compounding this threat, they were allowed to "wash and dress little white girls."[19] Asian immigration was likened to the "introduction in our school and nurseries of some new and horrible disease that defied treatment."[20]

Not only sexual diseases were associated with the Chinese, but also vile, unnatural, sexual practices. The threat of "300 million obscene yellow rascals" descending on the U.S., rapacious and insatiable "fiendish almond-eyed heathens" whose only goal was to deflower white girls: this slander predates American black-man-as-rapist hysteria and is later echoed in Nazi propaganda which showed slavering, taloned, dark-skinned Jews ravishing pure, "Aryan," frauleins. Newspapers printed endless stories sodden with race-mixing fears. Horace Greeley made no attempt to hide his revulsion: "The Chinese are uncivilized, unclean, and filthy beyond all conception without any of the higher domestic or social relations; lustful and sensual in their dispositions; every female is a prostitute of the basest order."[21]

Tales were widely published of "John Chinaman" attending Sunday School in order to get at white women. One teacher, who apparently escaped with her chastity intact, had, however, "her health broken down" by the overpowering reek of her Chinese students.[22] The *New*

York World, beneath the headline "Two Mongolian Minotaurs — Shocking Debauchery of Innocents," told of naïve adolescents lured into prostitution by Chinese laundrymen. Again and again American newspapers inflamed fears and hatred with lurid descriptions of white girls falling under the spell of opium and "Asiatic wiles." *The New York Times* in 1873 published a full page exposé of the city's Chinatown. It concentrated on Chinese "denizens continuously gambling, feasting on rodents, living in filth, and worshipping hideous idols." When a reporter asked the operator of an opium den about the "handsome but squalidly dressed young white girl" in his establishment, he replied "with a horrible leer 'Oh hard time in New York. Young girl hungry. Plenty come here. Chinaman always have something to eat, and he like young white girl, He! He!'"[23]

Horace Greeley, progenitor of the *New York Tribune*, helped
to perpetuate fear of and animosity towards the Chinese.
(Courtesy of Dictionary of American Portraits)

Thomas Edison, as developer of the kinetograph, was the first to exploit stereotypes of Chinese on film. His company produced a 1½-minute film called *Chinese Opium Den* in 1894. Ten years later he produced *Rube in an Opium Joint*, likely the earliest surviving film depicting drug use. Other exploitation and fear-mongering films followed: *Morphia — The Death Drug, Drug Traffic, Secret Sin, The Devil's Needle, Black Fear, The Girl Who Didn't Care*, and *The Devil's Assistant* — all made before 1920.[24]

Curiously, the theater itself was often seen as a place of drug-drenched sexual danger. "Hundreds of respectable girls" were supposedly drugged in dark movie houses by white slavers armed with secret poison needles. Other places where crowds congregated — amusement parks, street cars, music and dance halls — were also rumored to be haunted by hypodermic-wielding pimps.[25]

According to the tradition, New York's Chinatown prostitutes were predominantly white. The racial mixing stirred up a panicky response in law enforcement men, such as New York's police commissioner William McAdoo, who described Chinatown prostitutes as "the most wretched, degraded, and utterly vile lot of white women and girls that could be found anywhere."[26] On the West Coast, too, fears that Chinese were corrupting American youth ran high. San Francisco physician Winslow Anderson wrote of witnessing the "sickening sight of young white girls from sixteen to twenty years of age lying half-dressed on the floor or couches, smoking with their 'lover.' Men and women, Chinese and white people mix in Chinatown smoking houses."[27]

Folklore had it that the drug itself was equivalent to illicit sex: "many females are so much excited sexually by the smoking of opium during the first few weeks that old smokers with the sole object of ruining them have taught them how to smoke."[28]

The allegedly common practice of female slavery in American Chinese communities was also widely discussed. *The New York Times* in 1905, for instance, ran the story "Rescuing Angel of the Little Slaves of Chinatown," complete with illustrations of beautiful "brothel inmates" and Chinese procurers whipping them with the cat-o-nine-tails. The piece focused on the work of missionary Helen F. Clark, who "risked the murderous threats of enraged highbinders" in "the nether region of squalor and vice." Sensational tales of abduction, torture and moral decay dovetail neatly with the common association of Chinese and opium use. Sentimental at times, and occasionally dumb with disbelief, the *Times* reporter described the plight of a young slave girl in New York's Pell street.

> One day Miss Clark discovered little Ah Foon, discovered her in an opium den on a hank of matting by the side of her opium-soaked mother, who was molding pills for a score of depraved Chinamen to smoke. She was only seven years old and she was used for a runner for the opium joints.[29]

In "Chinese Slavery in America" Charles Holden too linked the debased sexual practices of the Chinese with their use of opium. And like the author of "Rescuing Angel," he seemed to take a perverse delight in describing bizarre tortures: "The life of the slave is a chapter telling of total debasement and ill treatment. The mission managers have found girls who have been burnt with red-hot irons, dragged about by the hair and had their eyes propped open with sticks."[30]

More common, however, was the image of women debauched by opium, willing sex-slaves to the bestial Chinese. Hamilton Wright, one of the most important figures in the legal attack on Asian drugs, noted that "one of the most unfortunate phases of the habit of smoking opium in this country is the large number of women who have become involved and were living as common-law wives or cohabiting with Chinese."[31]

Facts contradict this propaganda. Most white opium smokers were people of means: socialites, theatrical folk, financiers and other professionals. Though the habit was frequently associated with the criminal underclass, until the early 20th century it was still often a "gentleman's vice. White opium smokers of this period were generally described as 'sporting characters.'"[32]

A final thread in this knotted skein was pure American show biz. Chuck Connors, one of New York's most-quoted celebrity reconteurs, made a living in the 1890s as a "lobby gow," or tour guide, taking groups of well-heeled slummers into Chinatown. Novelists, royalty, and theatrical people, as well as run-of-the-mill wealthy gawkers, paid handsomely for an in-depth look at this "Chinese hell." There, Connors would spin tales of depravity and sin, identifying random passersby as "notorious Tong hatchet men," and women seen in upper story windows as "slave wives." Contributing much to the popular notion of the Chinese narcotic threat, he'd finally bring his charges to a fake opium den tricked out in the utmost of squalid Chinese decor. A man, named Georgie Yee, posed with a white woman as hopeless addicts. As a titillating climax to the tour, Yee would begin gibbering and jigging around the "den" — Connors explaining to his goggle-eyed guests that Yee's insanity was a direct result of the "demon opium." Lulu — Yee's consort — lounged lasciviously, as a potent reminder of how far white women could fall when they meddle with opium.[33] The fact that the entire episode was fabricated for tourists did not diminish its impact. The guests would flee back to their safe white enclaves and tell everyone they knew that they'd seen with their own eyes the effects of the demon flower.

American newspapers tirelessly editorialized
against the perceived threats of opium.

Sexual degradation, filth, disease, threats of racial degeneration, miscegenation and madness: taken together these elements formed a powerful, and long-lived, image in the American psyche. The Chinese — as carriers of the narcotic plague — stand as the first incarnation of the Dope Fiend, prototypical threat to American Purity.

4.

The sacrificial creature, or scapegoat, is one of the most ancient and deeply rooted figures in human consciousness. Whether animal or human, the scapegoat serves two crucial functions: the relief of intolerable anxiety, and the ritual purging of guilt. Few people in the industrialized world still believe in literal religious sacrifice, yet the archetypal patterns continue because the archetypal needs remain. The repression of unacceptable thoughts, desires, and impulses will continue as long as there is human culture. And one of the most basic results of this repression is the selection, condemnation and destruction of the scapegoat.

The term was coined in 1530 by biblical translator William Tyndale, his Anglicization of the Latin term *caper emissarus*. In *Leviticus 16*, we find a thorough description of this best-known sacrificial creature:

> When Aaron has finished performing the ritual to purify the Most Holy Place, the rest of the tent of the Lord's Presence, and the alter, he shall present to the Lord the live goat chosen for Azazel. He shall put both of his hands on the goat's head and confess over it all the evils, sins and rebellions of the people of Israel, and so transfer them to the goat's head. Then the goat chosen for Azazel shall be presented alive to the Lord and sent into the desert to Azazel in order to take away the sins of the people.[34]

This section of the Old Testament is concerned with ritual purity. Complex instructions are given to maintain the unpolluted status of Hebrew religious practice: dipping fingers into blood, ceremonial bathing, and the burning of animal fat, skin, meat and intestines.

The goat was, of course, later associated with the Devil in many traditions; Biblical scholars assume that the Azazel referred to here was a desert demon, or "the collective figure for all the desert spirits."[35] One element of this dynamic should be kept in mind: the best sacrificial creature, the one ordained by God, is also the most demonic. Christ, the lamb of God, bearer of the sins of humankind, is foreshadowed by Azazel's demonized goat. This is an excellent example of what Thomas Szasz calls the "cosmic recycling of vice into virtue, evil into good." The pattern of transformation goes in both directions: "to be a saint, one must start as a sinner." To be the Lord of all demons, one must start as the Greatest of Angels.[36]

Heroin, the most highly praised commercial medication of its time, fell to the status of the most reviled substance on earth within a few decades. The fact that most Americans are ignorant of heroin's birth and early halcyon years is no coincidence. Just as Satan's time as the Lord of Light, second only to God in greatness, is little-discussed now by those who believe in the Judeo-Christian tradition, so heroin's early life has been to a large degree erased from popular consciousness. Heroin as primal menace looms from the mists, its origin shrouded in rumor and half-truths. Knowledge of its development in the most modern pharmacological lab in the world works against the notion of the drug as filthy, polluting essence. Still, this conversion from white to black, from wonder drug to demon drug, conforms to the scapegoating pattern that can be found in most cultures, from prehistoric times to the present. As Europe and the U.S. passed through the Enlightenment and the

Industrial Revolution, many overtly religious sacrifices were discarded or transformed. With the widespread decline in "irrational" Christianity came an increased faith in "rational" science and technology. Nonetheless, people still needed scapegoats, and found them wherever they could.

For instance, consider the electric chair, first used only seven years before the introduction of heroin. In my book *Blood and Volts: Edison, Tesla and the Electric Chair,* I argue that capital punishment — particularly new execution techniques — serves the same function as ancient human sacrifice. The unacceptable, the "uncivilized" drives and wishes and ideas of a culture, are projected onto the criminal and then ritually expunged by taking his life. William Kemmler, the first man executed by the electric chair, was vilified during his trial as a drunken "hatchet fiend." Fifteen months later, as he was strapped into the electric chair, legal authorities and newsmen alike praised him as a scientific and societal paragon, transformed by the "godlike power" and "heavenly might" of electricity.[37]

Opium in the Middle Ages, alcohol in various forms, tea in China, sassafras during the 1500s, coffee and even tobacco smoke (inhaled or blown up the rectum in "gaseous clysters") were all at one time touted as cure-alls. Now they are highly suspect, if not strictly forbidden. Heroin leads the parade of substances once praised and now condemned. But as with other panaceas, its malign status is more a result of cultural upheaval than basic pharmacology.

"The purpose of the sacrifice is to restore harmony to the community, to reinforce the social fabric," René Girard writes in *Violence and the Sacred.* "The sacrifice serves to protect the entire community from its own violence; it prompts the entire community to choose victims outside itself."[38]

By a kind of sympathetic magic (using violent "treatment" to cure a violent "disease"), the most fearful members of a society strive to inflict the same pain that the supposed perpetrator has caused. Old Testament talion law is not so much about fairness or restoring moral balance as it is about undoing defilement. An act of antisocial violence contaminates every member of society; and eye for an eye gives the feeling of cleansing all taint. In the emotional heat of social chaos, members of the group seek an easy answer to their complex problems. Most social crises stem from tangled roots. Understanding these, let alone digging them out, is too difficult for most. A simple solution is desired. Even if the actual social chaos is not tamed, the feeling of chaos is reduced by acts of ritual violence. If Girard is correct, then violence directed at the sacrificial victim makes it both cursed and sacred. By blaming the scapegoat, society implicitly attributes to it miraculous or superhuman abilities. And by its expulsion or death, it evidences supernatural powers — healing the community's wounds.

The level of violence, the pitch of emotion accompanying the scapegoat ritual, is directly proportional to the level of phobic doubt that pervades a society. Dissent, factionalism, changes in racial and ethnic makeup, new beliefs (whether religious or scientific), technological innovation, economic uncertainty: all of these contribute to an intolerable sense of anxiety and turmoil. They often result in the demand for a scapegoat.

The period of heroin's demonization is often thought of as pure and idyllic. The so-called Gay Nineties, the

Aughts and Teens have been sentimentalized by film and popular fiction. But, in fact, this time was one of great fear and disruption in the U.S. Beside racial alarm and hygienic hysteria, a new discord convulsed the body politic: the Red Scare.

5.

In the year following World War One, the United States was gripped by a "national psychoneurosis."[39] Enemies were everywhere — or so the press screamed in ominous headlines. Wild-eyed anarchists, socialist saboteurs, bushy-headed Reds, Bolshevik revolutionaries bent on the wholesale destruction of the U.S. government: such were the specters which haunted the American psyche in 1919 and '20. The threat supposedly affected all aspects of national life, but the areas of labor and education were most rife with the "Red menace." The scare lasted little more than a year, culminating in the infamous Palmer Raids, with their sweeping abrogation of civil liberties and due process. But during that time, dozens were killed, thousands imprisoned and deported for alleged crimes against the state and the national soul. Most importantly for the story of heroin's fall, the Red Scare left Americans lusting for new scapegoats.

Emotions were still high after the defeat of Germany, and the threat of wartime saboteurs and sedition still haunted the country. A desire for normalcy and tranquillity also fed the mania for a national purge. In Russia, the Bolshevik Revolution raged, frightening the U.S. enough to send in its troops for the suppression of this threat to the status quo. Simultaneously, American radicals showed great enthusiasm for the revolution and Soviet goals. Bombs, sent through the mail, killed a few Americans, and one exploded on Wall Street in September of 1920. Riots flared — racial in Washington D.C., and union-related in Seattle and elsewhere. A number of new patriotic groups sprang up, or blossomed again: The

American Defense Society, National Security League, National Civic Federation, Better America Federation, Allied Patriotic Societies, National Patriotic Council, and the United States Patriotic Society. The American Legion was only surpassed by the KKK (reborn in 1915) in promoting patriotism. Klan membership exploded to 4,500,000 by 1924. Along with the American Legion, the Daughters of the American Revolution and the Hearst newspapers, the Klan howled for "100% Americanism." School textbooks were combed for unpatriotic messages, mandatory loyalty oaths were instituted for teachers, and calls for stricter immigration laws grew even more strident. The Klan's agenda was proclaimed clearly in 1926. It sought to eradicate "every girl-ruiner, every home-wrecker, every wife-beater, every dope-dealer, every moonshiner, every crooked politician, every pagan papist priest, every hyphenated-American, every lawless alien."[40]

Wide-spread outbreaks of labor unrest contributed to the air of anxiety. A steel strike, a coal miner's strike, and even a walk-out by Boston policemen convinced many Americans that the unions were conspiring to bring the country to ruin. The press — sniffing blood — pounced on these stories and ran amazingly biased reports. Calling radicals "assassins and madmen," "human scum," "crime-made beasts" and "vermin," the newspapers whipped American mobs to a frenzy. Editorial cartoons showed strikers as troglodytic rapists, wild-haired maniacs and murderers pouring liquid poison into the so-called Chalice of State.[41] But perhaps most important were the manipulations of public sentiment by a few self-serving capitalists. The owners of the coal mines and steel mills affected by the strikes had much to gain by painting union leaders as a toxin in the bloodstream of

America. Calvin Coolidge, then governor of Massachusetts, gained national fame and a path to the White House by repressing the Boston police strike. And A. Mitchell Palmer, the man who's most closely associated with the Red Scare, almost managed to parlay the national paranoia into a nomination for the presidency.

Calvin Coolidge, 30th president of the United States, gained fame as governor of Massachusetts by squelching a Boston police strike.
(Courtesy of Dictionary of American Portraits)

Born into a Quaker family, Palmer early on displayed a curious mixture of religious belief and cynical self-promotion. For political services rendered during Woodrow Wilson's run for the White House, he was rewarded with various posts. After serving as the Alien Property Custodian (he was instrumental in wresting control of the American Bayer plants and patents away from the parent German company), he was named attorney general. Noting the adoring press coverage that other Red-baiters had gotten, he instituted a series of raids against so-called Bolsheviks which stand as one of the nadirs of American justice. Hunting down aliens whom he believed to be a threat to the body politic, Palmer had thousands rounded up without arrest warrants, and held (without representation, hearing, or even charges) for days *incommunicado*. In filthy, ill-lit mass detention chambers with little food, miserable sanitation and at times no heat, the prisoners waited at Palmers' pleasure. When all was said and done, only a handful of real "radicals" were convicted or deported. Hundreds of those rounded up had absolutely nothing to do with "Bolshevistic" organizations. One ship was sent to the U.S.S.R. full of undesirable aliens; a few domestic true believers were convicted of fomenting division and strife. But a year later, when the country began to wake from its spell of paranoia, the purpose of the raids remained unclear.

To Palmer, however, this purge was not just a way of garnering publicity. He truly believed, or he convinced himself, that Reds were an infection in the bloodstream of America. In describing enemies caught in the raids, Palmer's social hygiene prejudices are obvious: "out of the sly and crafty eyes of many of them leap cupidity, cruelty, insanity, and crime, from their lopsided faces, sloping brows, and misshapen features may be recognized the unmistakable criminal type."[42]

It was not just a group of criminals who menaced the U.S. These were a genetic threat. Repeatedly — in newspapers, government proclamations, anti-labor propaganda — we can see this obsession with purity. One cartoon from the period shows Uncle Sam rooting out the virulent weeds of insurrection: fuzzy-headed, buck-toothed, "slope-browed," subhumans who sprout and breed and spread. Though Palmer focused most of his vitriol on social and political enemies, the "malicious racial cancer" was one ingredient in this stew of hate and fear. It may seem a great leap from the U.S. in 1920 to Nazi Germany in the 1930s, but there are a number of similarities between the Palmer raids and the persecution of the Jews. Both were predicated on racial/ethnic purification, both scapegoated a minority for expulsion, both were executed by agents of a legitimate national government, both now seem to be acts of madness. Of course, the Nazi atrocities caused far more suffering and death, but this may be attributable more to the degree of social disruption in Germany than to American law and decency.

The newspapers of William Randolph Hearst were another foul wind stoking the furnaces of hysteria. Hearst is generally credited with developing "yellow journalism." So powerful was his influence at the turn of the century that historians place the responsibility for the Spanish-American War squarely on his shoulders. Huge headlines, garish colors, wild and sensational illustrations, sentimentalism and paranoia in equal doses: the Hearst papers contributed much to the panicky atmosphere that choked the U.S. in the early 1900s. When Hearst's papers weren't detailing grisly lust-murders, illicit affairs, or tragedy and scandal, they were sounding a shrill alarm against the "yellow peril" of Asian immigration and the dangers of "voodoo satanic music" (jazz).

Publisher William Randolph Hearst's newspapers fanned the fires
of racism and scapegoating through yellow journalism.
(Courtesy of Dictionary of American Portraits)

Promoting a kind of Unified Dread Theory, Hearst's fear-mongering also included a long and unrelenting campaign against the "Dope Evil." Soon after the Red Scare abated, Hearst had his papers begin devoting a great deal of space to the threat of this new alien influence. In the 1920s and '30s he pushed his editors to publish articles that linked drugs with sordid crimes. Sensationalistic, overwrought, full of factual errors and bald fabrications, these articles had a major influence on the public's image of the Dope Fiend. Besides the "slant-eyed" heathen Chinese, Hearst targeted Mexicans for racial slander. After Pancho Villa took 800,000 acres of valuable land from him, Hearst had his papers run endless variations of the Mexican-as-drug-addled-menace tale. Interestingly, the term "marijuana" (previously Mexican slang for the plant) was promoted by Hearst as a way of associating the demon weed with Spanish-speaking immigrants. Before Hearst's hate campaign, the herb was sold in American pharmacies as Cannabis Indica or Indian Hemp. Screaming headlines warned readers of "Frankenstein monsters," "Bloodlust," "unparalleled viciousness" and "voodoo-satanic music" driving Fiends into bestial rampages. The so-called crime wave which Hearst's papers attributed to drugs included not only rape and murder but such outrages as blacks stepping on a white man's shadow, looking directly at white women, and laughing at whites.[43]

In one of the most overblown anti-drug screeds of the period, *Dope: the Story of the Living Dead*, Winifred Black wrote at length about the danger to the "white race" that opiates posed. Also known as Annie Laurie, Black worked for the Hearst chain for years, writing an advice column for the lovelorn. She's generally accepted as the first newspaper sob sister, precursor of all the Beatrice Fairfaxes and Miss Lonelyhearts. More importantly, she wrote hundreds of columns for Hearst on the "Dope Problem." Often accompanied by a photo of Black — a jowly, scowling schoolmarm — these articles were, by sheer volume and repetition, highly influential. "Unseen and Insidious, Drug Habit Creeps In," "60 Percent of All Convicts are Addicts," "Danger in Parole: Weak-kneed Judges at Fault," "Winifred Black Declares Dope Parley Farce," "Drug Ring Havoc," "U.S. Drug Slave Nation Says Authority," "Paradise Alley is Fetid Hell-Hole of Lost

Souls." Her articles recycle the same cliché and sentimental pabulum aimed especially at female readers.

> Dead — of morphine — the president of one of the biggest and best women's clubs in this city.
>
> Dead — of heroin — a writer known and beloved in every home in Illinois, a woman of refinement and culture.[44]

Dope, Black's book, is a delirious mixture of horror-mongering and breezy newspaper style. "Degradation, filth, disgrace, shame — what are these things but words, once you have grown to know the fitful fluttering of the black candle in your diseased brain?" The "living dead" are "ragged, dirty, half-insane, and absolutely helpless." And the menace to women was far worse than for men. The female "walking corpse doesn't comb her hair. She forgets her daily bath. She does not laugh. She is haggard, yellow-skinned, dull-eyed."[45]

Speaking directly to the female Dope Fiend, she conjures a picture of not only literal bad hygiene but eugenic degradation too. "You are back again in the dark and the dirt and the rags, with a black man on one side of you, stretched on the same couch and a yellow man too." The worst scenario Black can conceive is a race-mixing orgy, all social order broken down, all genetic barriers in ruins, the pure protoplasm of white women menaced by black and yellow pollutants. "Don't make any mistake about it — there's a dope peddler in your neighborhood — a Mexican, a Japanese, a Chinese, a negro."[46]

Harry J. Anslinger.
(Courtesy Historical Collections and Labor Archives,
Pennsylvania State University Library.)

Picking up the racist anti-dope torch and carrying it well into the 1950s was Harry Anslinger, head of the Federal Bureau of Narcotics. Though his obsession was more with marijuana (which he dubbed "the assassin of youth") than opiates, Anslingers' 32-year tenure as the nation's dope czar carried on the efforts of the social-hygienic crusaders of the early 20th century.

Tough, forthright, bearing an uncanny facial resemblance to Benito Mussolini, Anslinger was appointed head of the Bureau in 1930. A low-level diplomat during World War One, he came to the position with little experience in drug enforcement and none in medicine. His admirable record in the diplomatic corps was not his chief qualification to head the federal assault on narcotics, however. A deeply held belief in the menace of various ideologies (Communism, anarchism, socialism) enamored him with many congressmen. Equally important was the stamp of approval placed on him by W.R. Hearst.

To call Anslinger a racist is perhaps misleading. He made no statements regarding the inferiority of blacks, or argued that aliens had a devolutionary effect on the American gene pool. Still, the gospel he preached was heavy, near to collapse, with the burden of racist imagery. In 1937, for instance, he told Congress that "Negroes and Mexicans, and entertainers" were more likely to be Dope Fiends than whites. And their music — swing and bebop — was directly influenced by drugs. He told credulous congressmen that this "satanic music," in conjunction with drug use, lured white women into "sexual relations with Negroes." His hatred of jazz seemed to at times border on the pathological. He ordered his agents to keep files on a wide variety of musicians, from cutting-edge beboppers (Dizzy Gillespie and Thelonius Monk) to middle-of-the-road entertainers. Even such mainstream performers as Milton Berle and Andre Kostelanetz were secretly investigated for links to the Dope Evil. Anslinger's dream was a nationwide sweep of jazzmen, a once-and-for-all cleansing of this "syncopated taint." Likely impressed by the dispatch, if not the ruthlessness of the Palmer raids, Anslinger planned and plotted to round up in one dragnet all the blacks who threatened America's well-being with their "voodooistic" music.[47]

The anti-Bolshevik ideology that dominated his thinking in the 1920s was transformed, or merged with, the anti-narcotic beliefs crucial to his later policies. Anslinger appears to have ingested the Red Scare mind-set whole, and made it integral to his thinking. More than anyone else, America's extreme punitive stance toward drug use can be traced to Harry Anslinger. In his three decades as head of the F.B.N. he never once wavered from his belief that "severe mandatory prison sentences for first convictions" were the only defense against encroaching social pollutants.[48]

World War One and the Red Scare were a turning point for American consciousness, especially pertaining to foreign influence. Before the war, the usual explanation for America's drug appetite was to blame irresponsible doctors or the "American disease": extreme hurry and striving, a high-pitched and fast-paced life. But after the anti-German sentiment of World War One, after the Palmer raids, after Hearst's propaganda machine went into high gear and anti-Chinese slanders had thoroughly permeated American thinking, the blame for drug use was no longer placed on the citizens of the U.S. Scapegoats were needed; foreign powers and unscrupulous alien infiltrators were now labeled as the cause of America's drug use. Self-appointed narcotics experts — such as Hamilton Wright and congressman Stephen Porter — placed guilt on the malign influence of outsiders. From South America came cocaine. Heroin was a "German invention," shouted congressman Henry Rainey; and in the wake of the World War One, the term "German" evoked instant fear and suspicion. China sent crude opium. North Africa provided hashish. In short, the U.S. was surrounded by dangers on all sides. If America's "sacred germ plasm" was to be preserved, then constant vigilance, war-like self-defense, and perpetual surveillance would be necessary.[49]

6.

Richmond Pearson Hobson, who was instrumental in
the creation of the "Dope Fiend" stereotype.
(Courtesy of Dictionary of American Portraits)

Dope Fiend iconography can be traced to a wide variety of sources. But if responsibility for its final form and widespread dissemination is to be given to one person, it must be Richmond Pearson Hobson. According to William Weir, Hobson "single-handedly created the 'dope fiend,' a propaganda masterwork that ranks with the *Protocols of the Elders of Zion.*"[50] Racism, fear-mongering, pseudo-science, eugenic mania, self-aggrandizement, skillful manipulation of the media: these were all woven deeply into the career of Richmond P. Hobson. Interestingly, he wrote of the need for a "final solution" to the drug problem a year before *Mein Kampf* was published.[51] This is not to suggest that Hobson was an influence on Hitler, or was a crypto-fascist. My point is that both

American Dope Fiend paranoia and the German scape-goating of the Jews have significant connections. Two very different cultures, two distinct economic and political situations produced a surprisingly similar response during the same period.

Hobson began his career as a crusader speaking and writing against alcohol, which he claimed was a "protoplasm poison." The origin of his entire anti-dope philosophy can be found in his early anti-liquor work. *Alcohol and the Human Race* is a useful place to begin examining the various components that went into his thoughts, especially regarding the effects of drugs on procreation. Repressed sexual fears leak through in a hundred places in the book, like a relentless sea of reproductive anxiety surrounding a tiny boat. Sexual essence is epitomized as protoplasm — which he vaguely defined as composing the "physical machinery of all life and the evolution of all life in plants, animals and man." For Hobson, protoplasm was both physical and metaphysical, the essence of racial identity. In one place he described it as "sacred." Elsewhere, it is a mysterious "opaque jelly." He warned against a "destructive attack upon the glands of reproduction in men," conflated syphilis, gonorrhea and alcoholism, fretted about the fate of "the tender tissue associated with reproduction in male and female," and sounded the alarm against "withering blights on the germ plasm" which were "truly terrifying."[52] It doesn't require a professional psychological analysis to detect the sexual anxiety implicit in these claims, especially when we consider his admonitions about "brute Negroes" who "commit unnatural crimes" on white women.[53]

Hobson's book is a repetitive, pseudo-scientific attack on alcohol in all forms — blaming the Demon Rum for almost all of humankind's ills, including war, sexual perversion, venereal disease, lack of patriotism, political tyranny, "mob spirit, violence, rioting, incendiarism, anarchy, wanton destruction," low worker productivity and racial degeneration.[54] Like the Nazi racial philosophers who traced genealogies, Hobson argued at length that the blighting effects of liquor extended out to the fourth generation: "Thus having both parents and all four grandparents free from the poison and only one great-grandparent on one side alcoholized, nevertheless this generation was still degenerate." The effects were not merely physical disease, though. Hobson blamed the corrupting influence of alcohol for "mental deficiency, hysteria, convulsions, epilepsy, feeble-mindedness, idiocy or insanity," and claimed that drinkers often became "impulsive degenerates, criminals, profligates and moral imbeciles."[55]

For Hobson, it was always immorality and spiritual decay that lay at the heart of any social problem. Even as a youngster, stiff-necked Puritanism frequently colored his actions. He entered the U.S. Naval academy at age 14, and was nicknamed "Parson" for his sanctimonious attitudes and overpious behavior. His arrogance was manifested early and continued throughout his life. Though highly successful at organizing various anti-dope leagues, he tended not to work well with others. More than one writer has commented on his egotism and "powerful desire for individual recognition."[56]

A recent graduate from Annapolis, Captain Hobson made a name for himself during the Spanish-American War. When the Spanish fleet was at anchor in Santiago harbor, Hobson volunteered to take command of the coal-carrier *Merrimac* and scuttle it to keep the fleet bottled up. He was convinced that the Spanish gunners couldn't hit "anything smaller than the ocean."[57] Unfortunately, he overestimated their racial inferiority. The collier was sunk where it would do no good, and the brave American was fished out of the water. When Spanish Admiral Pascual Cervera greeted him and offered him liquor, Hobson made a fine show of refusing. Released from captivity a month later, Hobson returned to the U.S. a hero. Touring the country, he was exactly what a war-frenzied America wanted: a tall, handsome, soldier-hero "looking much like one of Frederick Remington's popular pictures of heavy-mustached cowboys."[58] At a welcoming ceremony in Chicago, a female cousin of Hobson's turned up and gave him a much-remarked-upon public kiss. Soon he was kissing hundreds of star-struck young women as he went from town to town. George Jean Nathan, of *The Smart Set*, claimed that Hobson was "the most dashing figure of romance for American women until the coming of Valentino." Completing his conversion into a popular culture icon, a candy-maker created the "Hobson Kiss" — a chewy confection that sold briskly wherever the hero appeared.

Hobson soon found that being a hero made him an instant expert. Marrying the daughter of a wealthy Wall Street banker, he was ready for the next, higher, step into public life. In 1906 Hobson won a congressional seat from his native Alabama and soon was working toward a total national ban on alcohol. In 1914, he was the first to call for a constitutional amendment for prohibition. Though defeated, Hobson's efforts set the stage for the coming victory of the Drys.

Andrew Sinclair provides an excellent analysis of the
deepest motivations driving the anti-liquor crusaders. In
Prohibition: the Era of Excess, he argues that the

> emotion which they exploited was fear: the fear of
> sin and God; the fear of race against race and skin
> against skin; the fear of venereal diseases; the fear
> of idiot children; the fear of violence suppressed by
> conscience and loosed by liquor; the dark sexual
> fears of civilization.[59]

And no one exploited these fears better than Richmond P. Hobson. He conceived of the history of mankind as the history of alcohol, no force having a greater
impact on evolution and the achievement of "higher civilization":

> In America we are making the last stand of the
> great white race, and substantially of the human
> race. If this destroyer can not be conquered in
> young America, it can not in any of the old and
> more degenerate nations. If America fails, the world
> will be undone and the human race will be
> doomed to go down from degeneracy into degen-
> eracy til the Almighty in wrath wipes the accursed
> thing out.[60]

Hobson remained in the public eye for decades: the
most well-known and well-received speaker on the subject of "protoplasm poison" and its analogue, racial degeneration. After achieving little of note in the House, he
was defeated in a run for the Senate in 1914 and devoted
the rest of his life to the crusade against bodily corruption. Allying himself with the powerful Anti-Saloon
League, Hobson traveled from city to city as the star lecturer. "Alcohol is killing our people at the rate of two

thousand a day, every day of the year," he told overflow audiences. Never constrained by facts or the need for documentation, Hobson made up statistics as he spoke. "One of five children of alcohol consumers is hopelessly insane." "Ninety-five percent of all acts and crimes of violence are committed by drunkards." "Nearly one half of all deaths that occur are due to alcohol." "One hundred and twenty-five million white men today are wounded by alcohol."[61]

Hobson's brag, that he was the highest paid lecturer in the U.S. (after William Jennings Bryan) is likely true. Between 1914 and 1922 he was paid $171,250 by the Anti-Saloon League. Hobson made $700 a week, plus $100 for every extra lecture he did.[62] He gave essentially the same speech, "The Great Destroyer," hundreds of times. But Hobson was not in the purity-and-pollution business just for the money. He believed his ceaseless propaganda. Giving the same speech, spouting made-up facts, looking out at thousands of eager faces in the audience, Hobson carved the tenets of his faith deeper and deeper into his own heart.

To call Hobson a racist is not very useful, as his brand of racial philosophy was far more complex than the average American prejudices of his time. In Hobson's thinking regarding race, he had absorbed much of the fear and hatred of the post-war Deep South. However, this doesn't explain completely the degree to which Hobson associated drug and alcohol use with "racial degeneracy." He was in favor of disfranchising blacks. Hobson spoke repeatedly about "the white man" being "further evolved" than blacks. He argued that white America needed to "clothe society with the mantle of protection, producing a race consciousness of this new peril." Hobson preached a gospel of instinctive "self-preservation, of race pride, of true patriotism" in which the "home, the state, the race," would protect itself against alien "scourges." Allied with the science of his day, his racism was more persuasive and long-lived than the crude name-calling that often characterizes racist propaganda.[63]

A bizarre notion of evolution and human destiny pervaded Hobson's thinking. He developed his concept of genetic progress — a "top brain/bottom brain" split — with little, if any, real scientific support. Still, Hobson repeated the theory endlessly and it was picked up and promoted by other writers. According to this theory, higher human functions were in the "top brain" or "shrine of the soul," while animalistic, anarchic, drives were in the "lower brain... where reside all the selfish instincts and impulses."[64]

Hobson made no clear distinction between alcohol and other drugs. For him, liquor was a "narcotic," so it was no leap at all to transfer the earlier warnings against alcohol to opiates. Thus a "narcotic promptly degenerates the red man, throws him back into savagery [and] will actually make a brute out of a Negro, causing him to commit unnatural crimes." More appalling, in Hobson's view, was the dire result of white men indulging. "Starting young, however it does not take a very long time to speedily cause a man in the forefront of civilization to pass through the successive stages and become semicivilized, semisavage, savage, and, at last, below the brute."[65]

Devolution and degeneracy were a threat most acutely felt in the U.S. because "we believe this American civilization to be the highest type, yet the United States is the most dope-ridden nation of all." Serious measures needed to be taken to prevent a slide into protoplasmic barbarism and to ensure "the unimpeded progress of America, of the race itself."[66]

This is not merely a genetic mandate, but the will of God Himself. Hobson's anti-dope rhetoric was laden with religious imagery. For every American, the war against dope was not mere individual struggle, but affected "his family, his country, the evolution of human life and the destiny of Man and the will of God in Creation."[67]

Hobson referred to drug use as "sin," recommended "preaching" the "gospel of narcotic abstinence," and proposed a strange theory of cure: "The grace of God provides the impulse that sends the blood current back into the upper brain to restore destroyed tissue and reawaken the higher impulses." And echoing the angel-to-devil motif we've repeatedly seen, he claimed that a drug "once supposed to be the 'water of life'" was in reality a lethal poison, a deadly threat to the "sacred germ plasm."[68]

Hobson's campaigning was perhaps more effective than he'd hoped. Three years after Congress defeated his anti-alcohol resolution, it passed the Volstead Act. Hardly different than the measure he'd proposed, it outlawed the manufacture, sale and transport of liquor in the U.S. Suddenly, Hobson was robbed of the enemy he'd built his life around. Having taken the role of prophet (*Time* later called him the "Joshua in the Jericho of Dope."[69]) he needed a new foe. Less than a year after Prohibition went into effect, he made his first formal move against dope, publishing a 25-page booklet, *The Perils of Narcotics.*

By 1923, drugs had become Hobson's primary interest; that year he organized the International Narcotic Education League and was immediately elected president. One of his earliest attempts to rouse public furor against the "dope evil" was a proposed "saturation attack on the nation's youth." Hobson asked Congress to publish 50,000,000 copies of his pamphlet at public expense. Congress declined, the cost being prohibitive.

During the 1924 presidential campaign, Hobson was more successful, pressing the candidates to support his plans. Both parties included anti-dope planks in their platforms. Two years later he formed the Narcotics Defense League and the World Conference on Narcotics Education. In 1927 Hobson formed the World Narcotics Defense Association. Besides his own organizations, he convinced other groups — such as the National Federation of Women's Clubs, the Knights of Columbus, the Elks, Moose and a number of Masonic Lodges — to join the crusades against heroin.[70] After the anti-German hysteria of World War One had abated and the Red Scare had been to a certain degree forgotten, Americans were eager for a new enemy. Hobson's efforts provided a convenient menace for clubs and organizations which felt a need for a new, or a more compelling, reason for being. Noncontroversial — who would defend the demon heroin? — dope provided an easy target.

Living well, spending freely, Hobson devoted much of his effort to fund-raising. He received money from various philanthropic sources, including Josiah Lilly, and after his death, Lilly's sons. Besides fighting heroin, Hobson and the pharmaceutical giant worked together to have the cocaine removed from Coca Cola. Hobson also solicited funds from Henry Ford. But because Ford insisted that tobacco be added to the list of demonic substances, and Hobson as a Southerner refused, no Ford money was forthcoming. Though the Depression put a serious crimp in his fund-raising, Hobson managed to spend the rest of his life fighting the evils of heroin. By the time of his death (in 1937), his efforts had paid off. Heroin was utterly demonized, and a new drug, cannabis, was rising in public consciousness to take its place as the new menace.

Through speeches, lobbying, efforts to change textbooks, his own publications, interviews, sermons and magazine writing, Hobson more than any other person succeeded in fusing forever the notion of opiate "addiction" and violent criminality.

The image Hobson created was complex. On one hand he claimed that opiates gave the user an exaggerated sense of self. "Under the influence of the drug he becomes a heroin hero. He will do anything, he will dare anything. Or without it, he will do anything to get it."[71] At the same time the user is a degraded wretch. In order to supply his need he will

> lie, steal, rob if necessary, commit murder. Heroin addiction can be likened to contagion. Suppose it were announced that there were a million lepers among our people. Think what a shock the announcement would produce! Yet drug addiction is far more incurable than leprosy, far more tragic to its victims, and is spreading like a moral and physical scourge.
>
> There are symptoms breaking out all over our country and now breaking out in many parts of Europe which show that individual nations and the whole world are menaced by this appalling foe...

marching to the capture and destruction of the whole world.

Most of the daylight robberies, daring holdups, cruel murders and similar crimes of violence are now known to be committed chiefly by drug addicts, who constitute the primary cause of our alarming crime wave.

Drug addiction is more communicable and less curable than leprosy. Drug addicts are the principle carriers of vice, diseases, and with their lowered resistance, are incubators and carriers of the streptococcus, pneumococcus, the germ of flu, of tuberculosis and other diseases.

Upon the issue hangs the perpetuation of civilization, the destiny of the world and the future of the human race.[72]

Worse even than contagion, degeneration, murder and rape, according to Hobson, was the threat that heroin posed to the youth of America. He repeated endless reports of children snared by the demon drug. Heroin "catches the boy and girl between 16 and 20, or even younger, like the young bird before it has learned to fly." Only one taste and a minor lawbreaker becomes a "desperado of the most vicious type." The metaphor of contagious disease appeared especially often when he wrote about children. "With the spread of heroin over the land, an army of our youth has turned into daring criminals. Each one multiplying himself by bringing other youths into addiction."[73]

The image of the festering social sore spewing infectious germs recurs endlessly, sounding more like a sensationalistic horror story than a rational examination of a societal problem. Hobson's claims, at times, beggar belief. For instance, black users "degenerate to the level of the cannibal." The title of his 1933 book, *Drug Addiction: A Malignant Racial Cancer* echoes the xenophobia and hysterical dreads of Hobson's contemporary and spiritual ally, H.P. Lovecraft. "The Crawling Chaos," "The Lurking Fear," "The Unnamable" — these might be Hobson's terms. In fact, they're grotesque horror stories which appeared on newsstands at exactly the same time that Hobson was railing against "lepers," "moral and physical scourges," "perverts," "degenerate Negroes," and "racial cancers." It may be coincidence that Hobson began his anti-dope career the same year that *Weird Tales* appeared first on the newsstands, but there are remarkable similarities between his propaganda and the stories and illustrations in America's premier magazine of fear, disgust and titillating gore. Hobson called heroin a "Frankenstein monster" created by German scientists. And the defining image of his 1927 broadcast, "The Living Dead," clearly evokes the atmosphere of the Gothic tale.[74]

The year before, Sara Graham-Mulhall, strongly influenced by Hobson's hysteria, expounded at great length about "opium vampires" in her book *Opium: the Demon Flower.* "Human monsters" preyed on innocent white girls, "American born, daughters of good families, young women of intelligence and breeding." Even Hobson's assertion that religious conversion may be the "addict's only hope of freedom" echoes the vampire myth.[75]

Hobson's fear-mongering reached its zenith in ludicrous tales of opiates "inclosed in hot dog sandwiches and ice cream cones" and heroin-laced toiletries. "In using any brand of face powder regularly, it is a wise precaution to have a sample tested for heroin." Archetypal images of American youth and innocence are endlessly exploited; in an interview he told the unsubstantiated tale of a mother injecting her eight-year-old son with morphine, merely because the "addict" has a mania to create more "addicts." Girls lured into drug-slavery by the use of opiate "headache powders," gun-wielding teenaged maniacs, "snow gangs" terrorizing schools and rampaging through peaceful little towns: these are the images that Hobson incessantly repeated in the media. Not surprisingly, he seldom cited sources for his outrageous claims.[76]

Depending, apparently, upon whim, he variously claimed that there were 200,000, one million or even four million "drug addicts" in the U.S. Equally unreliable was his assertion that "90 percent of the crime committed" in Los Angeles was "traceable to narcotics." One of his most grievous manipulations of statistics was the frequently repeated claim that there'd been a 900 percent increase in "drug addiction" between 1919 and 1920. This was based on an increase from one to nine percent of the drug-using population of Sing Sing prison. This, obviously, was hardly a broad or representative sample to base such sweeping assertions on. Nonetheless, others took up the claim and it entered the drug-addiction mythology of the day. Even the journal of the A.M.A. — not well known at this time for objectivity or unbiased reporting — publicly chastised Hobson for "distortions and exaggerations."[77]

Ultimately, though, it's not Hobson's disregard for statistical accuracy or scientific process that so corrupted his work. It is the fact that he was first and foremost a religious zealot. Using the "say it often enough and people will believe it" technique, he devoted the last 20 years of his life to promoting an image of drug use that shows no sign of weakening, even a half-century after his death. His ideology of purity came before fact; his racist doctrines took precedence over clear-headed analysis; his bizarre theories of evolution and brain physiology had greater import for him than rational examination of evidence; his panic-stricken psycho-sexual dogma was far more compelling to him — and his followers — than would have been the testimony of 1,000 actual opiate users. More similar to a Roman Catholic inquisitor — rooting out spiritual evil — than a scientist, Hobson has a distinguished place in the pantheon of American propagandists.

7.

The efforts of Richmond P. Hobson and others like him were successful. In the years between World War One and the end of Prohibition, the gospel of the dope menace became the national orthodoxy: preached from pulpits, in the halls of Congress and state legislatures, on the radio and given increasing amounts of space in newspapers, especially the powerful Hearst chain.

Before Hobson had begun his crusade, the Federal government had estimated the number of "addicts" in the U.S. at 1,000,000.[78] This statistic, apparently a compromise between the Public Health Service and the Revenue Service, became the base of much anti-dope propaganda. With the added impetus of steadily mounting fear-mongering, the number of "addicts" rose, at least in public perception. Some voices of sanity and objectivity argued against the grossly inflated figures. For instance, Dr. Alexander Lambert called the numbers bandied about by the anti-dope forces "enormously exaggerated." But he was in a distinct minority. Estimates as high as 5,000,000 were published. In New York City alone, according to *The World*, there were 200,000 Dope Fiends. Frederic Wallis echoed this figure ten years later, claiming that there were "200,000 drug addicts of the underworld type" in New York City alone.[79]

How many opiate users were there really in the U.S. at this time? Lawrence Kolb and A.G. De Mez concluded that the number of users had peaked between 1890 and 1909, and then began to decline to approximately 100,000 — nationwide — by the mid-1920s. David Musto also argues that opiate users in the U.S. peaked about 1900 at a number somewhere between 200,000 and 400,000. Then it declined through the first three decades of the century. New laws, more stringent enforcement, the death of many older users, the decline in iatrogenic dependence, and other factors caused the use of opiates in the U.S. to decrease, all the while dope-panic was rising to ever higher levels.[80]

In addition to the influence of anti-dope crusaders, the changing demographics for users also influenced the climate of opinion. Older, female, middle-class users were being replaced by an increasingly male, younger, group. In New York City, generally accepted as the place where newer Fiends began to appear en masse, many users were switching from morphine to heroin.[81] Roughly 20 years after its introduction, heroin overcame its parent drug in popularity — at least in New York. David Musto examined admission records for Bellevue Hospital and found that 1915 was the first year when heroin users outnumbered morphinists.[82]

In *The American Disease*, Musto traces the origins and early ramifications of narcotic control in the U.S. This work is unsurpassed for accuracy, thoroughness and objectivity. I recommend it to any serious student of the subject; there is no need here to go over in detail what Musto has examined so exhaustively. But a brief overview of the legal response to opiates will be useful before returning to a discussion of the full flowering of hysteria and panic surrounding drugs.

In the years leading up to World War One, there had been a rising clamor for a tighter grip on drugs. The U.S. Pure Food and Drug Act of 1906 was a serious blow to the patent medicine business, requiring labeling of all medicines which contained opiates or cocaine. Still, as the perception of a drug epidemic grew, voices shouted for increased control. Various international congresses and conferences were held in hopes that world-wide control of drugs could be achieved. Producer nations were pressured to clamp down. At this time, the U.S. drug policy was a glass house, and a number of Americans — notably Charles Brent and Hamilton Wright — were already throwing stones. Largely as a sign of good faith to other countries — putting its own house in order — the U.S. Congress passed the Harrison Act which went into effect in March, 1915. The law contained three major provisions. First was the requirement that producers and distributors of narcotics register themselves and provide records to the Federal government regarding their activities. Secondly, a tax was levied on all sellers and producers of controlled substances. Thirdly, the Act required that anyone not registered with the government needed a prescription for "legitimate medical purposes" in order to buy or possess the drugs in question. The user was thus placed in a position of dependence on the medical profession, which was in turn controlled by Washington. As the Harrison Act was nominally a revenue measure, Federal Treasury agents were charged with enforcement. By June of 1916, 124,000 doctors, 47,000 pharmacists, 37,000 dentists, 11,000 veterinarians and 1,600 producers and wholesalers were registered with the Bureau of Internal Revenue.[83]

Two results were soon noticed: users began to switch from sniffing heroin to injecting it, and the price of the drug increased 1,500 percent. In the years of legal heroin, the vast majority of users took the drug by sniffing. It was then of a very high purity, and the desired effect was obtainable without resorting to the needle. As sup-

plies dried up, clandestine distributors began to adulter-
ate the drug. In order to get the same effect, heroinists
first began inter-muscular injection, then intravenous
mainlining.

At the same time, the price of heroin increased by a
factor of 15. According to one source, the cost of heroin
on the street went from $6.50 an ounce to $100 an
ounce as a result of the Harrison Act.[84] A writer for *The
New Republic* reported that in 1916 the price of heroin
went from 85¢ a dram to seven dollars a dram, and this
was adulterated to the point where injection was necessary to get a satisfactory result. An additional pressure
was the 1909 ban on smoking opium, which had sent
habitué in search of an affordable substitute.[85]

Certain forces within the U.S. — local, state and federal — were sympathetic to the plight of heroinists. Used
to cheap, safe and easily available drugs, they were suddenly thrown on the mercy of street dealers. Since 1912,
there had been, on a small scale, clinics to provide opiates and cocaine to those with dependencies. In 1919, as
the hysteria regarding drug use and "foreign elements" in
the U.S. increased, the Internal Revenue Bureau recommended that more maintenance clinics be opened. The
hope was that by providing drugs in a safe and regulated
environment crime would be reduced and the impetus
for the black market eliminated. Forty-four clinics
opened eventually, in cities as varied as New York and
Shreveport, San Diego, Cleveland, Memphis, Houston
and Paducah, Kentucky. Unfortunately, these clinics
rapidly fell afoul of public opinion and federal authorities. Though many were well run, serving thousands of
users, others — such as the one in Albany, New York —
were tainted by graft. But the primary reason for the

clinics' short life was the rising anti-dope sentiment. At the height of the Red Scare, few people were willing to defend such a questionable practice as providing free drugs. Photos in newspapers of Dope Fiends lining up for their daily dosage offended the sensibilities of many Americans. Soon, the Narcotics unit of the Treasury Department began to shut them down. A variety of Supreme Court rulings also strengthened the anti-maintenance forces. The experiment was largely over by 1921.

In New York City, a number of public officials pledged allegiance to the anti-dope orthodoxy. Frederic Wallis, the city's Commissioner of Correction, summed up the mounting frenzy in "The Menace of the Drug Addict." Drug use, for him, was synonymous with crime. "All drug addicts are criminals, either actual or potential, and there is no limit to their atrocities." The gross excesses of law enforcement agents during the Palmer Raids were apparently of little import: "No measure is too radical or severe that would prohibit the manufacture and sale of habit-forming drugs." The nation, the most elevated members of the human race, had a mandate to stop illicit drug use at any cost: "The greatest menace confronting civilization today is drug addiction."[86] Dr. Dana Hubbard, an officer of the City Health Department, also sounded the warning: "Heroin used by a human being produces an unmoral savage."[87] Mayor John Hylan appointed an investigative committee to examine the supposed connection between heroin use among the young and anarchist bombings of public institutions and leaders.[88]

Not only New York, which did in fact have the highest number of heroinists in the U.S., but the entire nation believed that a "crime wave" driven by drugs was sweeping America. Almost every state in the union, and many cities, passed stringent anti-dope laws. Endless repetitions of the supposed link between opiate use and criminality bombarded the populace. But in the main, these were examples of circular reasoning: drugs were illegal, drugs users were arrested and sent to prison; therefore drugs caused crime.

In 1924, congressman Stephen G. Porter introduced a bill to ban the import of opium for the production of heroin. After hearings in which new misinformation was given a public forum (e.g.: "Heroin addicts spring from sin and crime," "heroin contains, physiologically, the double action of cocaine and morphine."[89]), Congress enacted a national ban on the manufacture of heroin. That same year, the last maintenance clinic was shut down. Thus, 26 years after it was introduced, heroin had made an almost complete transformation. The 1924 law prohibited heroin except under very limited conditions; it was still possible — though extremely difficult — for hospitals and physicians to use heroin. Not until 1956 was heroin's demonization complete. In that year, heroin was declared by the federal government to be contraband in any and all circumstances, subject to seizure by the police: utterly anathema.

8.

By the time Prohibition was repealed, dope and the Dope Fiend had become as firmly fixed in the American popular consciousness as the blood-mad red Indian, the cruelly brilliant German scientist, or the crazed Red saboteur. Looking closely at the newspaper illustrations and editorial cartoons of the 1930s and '40s provides insight into the emotional content of the dope menace as it took its final form.

The images fall into four categories: 1) animal/vermin, 2) mythological creatures, 3) human forms, 4) animated objects.

The first and most common representation of dope was as an animal. The snake with multiple heads, slant-eyed (echoing the fear of the Chinese), fork-tongued, ready to strike. The jackal who holds a beautiful woman between his savage teeth, whose furious eyes stare back at the reader unafraid and unrepentant. The bat with teeth bared. The raging King Kong-like ape. One image of dope-as-spider includes the dark-eyed, fanged "Jewish" face so common in Nazi propaganda. A sphinx-like cat whose eyes shine balefully, and the vicious dog represented dope. The last animal image to consider was the vulture. with his hook-like jaw, wrinkled neck, talons splayed, perched on a bone, feeding its brood of vul-turettes, he was an effective image for the drug menace ready to swoop down and pick the bones of the "living dead."

Next are the mythological creatures. Artists depicted dope as the Grim Reaper picking flowers in a field of skull-headed poppies (see page 143). His grin and sickle, his cowl and boney grasp, are the stuff of cliché. But the endless field of death's-head poppies was a new twist on a hoary image. Demons of course were used, with all the traditional trappings: beard, horns, hooves, bat wings, snakey tail coiled around goat legs, and in at least one version, the hooked nose so common in anti-Jewish slanders. With bulging eyes, claws and fangs, the dragon also stood for dope. And the witch of Halloween lore made an appearance, too.

Dope as a demon.

Dope in human form as the "Big Man"; i.e. John Bull.

Less fantastic human figures crop up also: the thug with cap and tie and jutting jaw, the "Chinaman" villain of film and pulp fiction (bald, slavering, grasping at white women with taloned hands). A fat man in spats, formal suit, white gloves and top hat often represented the "Big Man" of the dope ring: successful, wealthy, and untouchable by the law. His resemblance to John Bull may be an echo of American resentment regarding British involvement in the opium trade. A final human figure is the cave man, complete with club and fur breech cloth. The opposite of the Big Man, the Neanderthal was used to depict the stupidity of drug use, and the devolutionary effect that drugs had on the user.

Dope personified as an animated object.

Lastly, artists personified dope in illustrations by putting arms and legs and a skull-head on a bottle. In one picture, dope leads another skeletal figure (with smoking pistol) in an attack on American youth.

The symbolic content of these images is not simple. Dope and the Dope Fiend were paradoxically less than human (verminous) and greater than human (powerful, supernatural). The most common type of image was the animal, particularly the predator. This image fits in well with the generally accepted notion of the scapegoat: outside of the group, disconnected so that his death or expulsion will not necessitate revenge.

Creature of darkness: bat and snake. Eaters of carrion: jackal and vulture. Cunningly patient: the spider and cat. These images of the Dope Fiend play on our anxieties. The Grim Reaper, demons and dragons touch deep and irrationally parts of our psyche. And this is crucial. The war against the Dope Fiend was fought, and continues to be fought, largely in the realm of the irrational. Fact was often crushed by more compelling fiction; logical analysis was frequently buried under automatic emotional response. The use of these sensationalistic images, and the often irrational verbal expression of propagandists such as Hobson and Anslinger, had a far greater impact on the American notion of drug use than objective examination. Or perhaps a completely rational discussion of this topic is, in fact, impossible. Any edifice built on such an irrational foundation may be beyond reason. Like capital punishment, abortion, and gun rights, the subject of drugs may be one that is more about emotion and psychological need than fact. And this gives the symbolic content of the images even more importance.

At no point in this book have I argued that heroin's properties are entirely symbolic. Of course there are measurable physiological effects from the drug. But my concern is more with the nonrational, emblematic nature of heroin, which I believe to be far more important for our understanding of its place in our cultural pantheon than its chemical properties.

Some will disagree, claiming that "mere" symbolic content is trivial. But consider certain other highly-charged substances, for instance kosher wine and holy water.

> Although it would be idiotic to look for the property of kosherness in wine, or for the property of holiness in water, this does not mean that there is no such thing as kosher wine or holy water. Kosher wine is wine that is ritually clean according to Jewish law. Holy water is water blessed by a Catholic priest. This creates a certain demand for such wine and water by people who want this sort of thing; at the same time, and for precisely the same reason, such wine and water are rejected by those who do not believe in their use.[90]

Holy water does have actual physical properties; it can quench thirst, put out a fire, irrigate a garden. But of course these are not the uses it is put to. Likewise, kosher wine can be used by non-Jews for purposes other than Jewish ritual (and in fact one brand of this type of wine is known among alcoholics and teenagers as "Mad Dog"). Consider also the cross — two pieces of wood fastened at their midpoint — and the furor that ensured when an artist dipped a cross in urine. An even more extreme example is the uses to which the American flag is put. One could argue that it's only a rectangle of colored cloth. Yet tempers flare, and politicians rail and foam, when the American flag is not treated with ceremonial respect.

Do most Americans say the flag is "just" a symbol? Hardly. Thousands have died for symbols: the swastika, the stars and stripes, the stars and bars, the fasces, the hammer and sickle, the cross, the crescent, the Star of David. Kiss a religious icon or a flag — or spit on it — and there's little to distinguish these two acts (mouth, saliva, intimacy). Yet the responses evoked by these two acts could hardly be less alike.

Similarly, I would argue, heroin is largely a symbolic substance: invested by cynical and well-meaning people alike with a heavy burden of meaning far beyond the chemical properties of a certain opiate alkaloid.

One of the most striking — and inarguable — characteristics of heroin is its ability to kill pain. Yet since 1956, heroin has been absolutely forbidden to American doctors and hospitals, even those treating patients in extreme and unrelenting pain. This is the case because of heroin's symbolic, not medical, properties.

America's highly ambiguous response to pain is made patently clear in its struggle against heroin. The "no pain, no gain" dogma was part of American orthodoxy long before body-builders took it up. The word "indolent" was often used to denigrate the drug user in the early 20th century. It now has, in general usage, a wholly negative meaning: lazy, self-satisfied, the opposite of the can-do, hard-working pioneer spirit. But in medical terminology it retains its original meaning: causing no pain. Heroin was likely named after heroic therapy, yet it posed a threat to the long-standing notion of salvation-through-pain. Often propagandists such as Hobson and Anslinger wove hellish imagery into their screeds — opiates as infernal torment. And certainly heroin users deprived of their drug experience intense suffering. Yet it seems to me that Hobson, Anslinger et. al. were concerned more about infernal pleasure then the torments heroinists endured. I'm convinced Dope Fiend crusaders were more appalled by the indolence of users than they were by its potential for causing suffering. And certainly their hateful imagery evidences little sympathy for men and women racked by the agonies of withdrawal.

Heroin's little brother, aspirin, was accepted wholeheartedly. It spawned numerous other over-the-counter pain killers which now sell in the billions each year. Strangely, American are seen by the rest of the world as big babies (who must have everything their way, who swallow millions of pills each year to blunt their minor sufferings) who are yet still deeply attached to the "no pain, no gain" philosophy.

Indolence, laziness, self-indulgence, irresponsible pleasure-seeking: most scapegoated groups in America have been slandered with these accusations. Blacks, Chinese, Spanish-speaking Americans, Indians, Irish, and southern Europeans were all at one time tarred with this brush. Dovetailing with these slurs was also the belief that these groups were "backward and uncivilized." Heroin, though at the time the ultimate in pharmacological progress, was quickly recast as an agent of regression, devolution, sloth and anti-American sentiment. Another link in this chain was the notion that "primitives" were more erotically indulgent than the so-called higher races. It's no surprise then that opiates were consistently associated with sex. White slavers, men of leisure and ladies of pleasure, Chinese pimps, black rapists — the sensationalistic reports of the early 20th century frequently linked illicit sex and heroin. And as David Musto points out, "Inordinate pleasure caused by drugs, moreover, was

seen to provide youth with a poor foundation for character development, and a resulting loss of independence
and productivity."[91]

In contrast to "foreign" opiates, alcohol was perceived
— once the forces of Prohibition were defeated — as native and natural. Dr. Stille summed up the idea this way:

> It is true that opium is not likely to become popular
> among industrious races like the Anglo-Saxon,
> whose preference must always be far more the po-
> tent, though less permanent, stimulus of ardent
> spirits, the gross and mortal enjoyments of which
> are far more suitable to the character of the race
> than the divine luxuries of opium.[92]

Alcohol was, and still largely is, associated with the
competitive spirit, action, manliness, and strength. Opiates in comparison were thought to engender narcissism,
inefficiency, defeatist and self-centered behaviors, low
productivity, regression and anti-social violence. Perhaps
they also stir up such powerful emotion because they cut
to the heart of the most American of notions: freedom.
The Dope Fiend is a "slave," yet by his choice of drugs he
proclaims his preference to opt out of the mainstream
society. His refusal to place social good before personal
desire brings to the surface many of the repressed contradictions in America's doctrine of freedom. Is choosing
to be enslaved an act of freedom? Is the normative, status
quo life just one more kind of slavery?

Similarly, the contradictions of male/female roles also
can be found in symbolism of the "addict." Though the
Dope Fiend was almost always pictured as being male,
the drug habit itself was frequently tinctured with femaleness. Crusaders spoke of opiates unmanning a man,

making him weak, dependent, and slavish. Certainly there was some holdover from the older stereotypical opiate user: the helpless, self-indulgent, middle-class woman. The "femaleness" of the Dope Fiend is only a flavor, one more ingredient in the symbolic stew. Like most enduring popular cultural figures, the Dope Fiend does not have a single source. Though aggressive, violent, immoral and powerful, there remains a shadow of the tainted female within him. And the preoccupation with the menace to white women, whether from blacks, Mexicans, Asians, or more generic degenerates, may be a perverse echo of the anxiety that "female taint" so often stirs up.

It would be simplistic to attribute American's obsession with the dark-skinned Other to one cause, or to use only one explanatory model, such as Freudian theory. Nonetheless, there are deep and long-standing wounds in the American soul. Guilt is one of the most difficult emotions to purge. It's possible that Americans' collective guilt — over slavery, over the genocide of the Indians, over the exploitation of immigrants — manifests itself as the dark-skinned Other. More than one writer has called the U.S. a haunted place, not literally haunted by ghosts, but by ghostly forces and memories, with regret and guilt flickering at the corner of the eye. They are impossible to lay to rest. Repression puts them down for a while, but they eventually return, stronger and in new forms.

The wild Indian — skulking in the forest, naked, face painted, as eager to rip off a white man's scalp as to press his dark finger prints on virginal white flesh. Is he a ghost returned to make our sleep uneasy? The black rebel — from Nat Turner to Superfly, strong, violent, attractive, menacing, refusing to submit to the white man's game. Though these figures of black independence were not produced directly by whites, certainly white oppression and exclusion were a major force in their development. Are they spectral manifestations of American guilt? The grasping, taloned, inscrutable Asian — the British fear him as Dr. Fu Manchu and Dr. No. America has given him no distinctive name, but we see him in collective dreams (films, novels, newspapers, comic books) reaching out to steal, ravish, and defile. In the 1990s a new version of the dark-skinned Other came forward: the Islamic "terrorist," crazed and suidically violent.

Black, red, brown and yellow; an uneasy mixture of indolence and supernal strength, stupidity and cunning, ugliness and sexual allure, childish spite and the decadence of old age; the image is that of a fiend. And the echoes, all the way back to the Black Shining Man (as the witch-haunted Salamites called the Devil), are remarkable.

First, the Dope Fiend as demonic menace is obsessed with recruitment. "A heroin addict has literally a mania to lead others into addiction and will make every effort to do so, having no pity even for children." warned Richmond Hobson.[93] Like the Dope Fiend, the Devil, too, is of course a tempter: secretive, threatening when he needs to be, sweet and wheedling when that serves his purposes. A newspaper editorial from 1925 merged the two into one: "And frequently, sinking to the lowest depths, his degradation takes the form of seeking with malicious Satanic ingenuity to inflict the drug curse upon others."[94]

In the popular iconography of the Devil, there is a pact. The terrified people of Salem testified against the Devil, "the grand Seignior of Hell, that mighty tyrant," claiming that he demanded they sign his book of damnation.[95]

> The Devil, exhibiting himself ordinarily as a small black man, had decoyed a fearful knot of proud, froward, ignorant, envious and malicious creatures to lift themselves in his horrid service by entering their names in a book by him tendered unto them.[96]

Both the addict and the Devil, according to folklore, are powerfully seductive. "Just make your mark here... just one little taste of heroin." The dynamic is almost identical: an unholy covenant that binds the recruit to an eternity of torment. "The chief obsession of the drug addict," stated Dr. Mackin in 1919, "is to gain converts to the cult."[97]

Take the stealth of the Indian, the cruel genius of the "oriental," the literal black skin and figurative black heart of the African, mix well in a cauldron heated by political turmoil and environmental threat, and you have the image of the Devil who stalked New England in the 1600s. Take the same ingredients and similar atmosphere of social upheaval, and you have the Dope Fiend of the early 20th century.

The seducer and the victim of seduction are the same. Just as opiates were supposed to be a devolutionary force, creating degenerate beasts from ordinary citizens, so too the Devil — in his assault on the Puritan colony — was accused of "transforming those wretches into Brutes and Birds," as Cotton Mather reported.[98] And like the great army of addicts which Hobson claimed was spreading over America "more destructive and biologically more dangerous" than actual armed attack, likewise

Satan's forces, "a vast power or army of Evil Spirits," had been gathered together to reclaim the Puritan outpost from the hand of God.[99]

Notes:

1. Girard, René. *Violence and the Sacred.* (Baltimore, Maryland: John Hopkins U.P.) 1977. p. 13.
2. *Missionary Herald.* LXXII. (1876) p. 30.
3. Gutzlaff, Charles, in: *Chinese Repository I* (1832) p. 126.
4. Williams, Samuel. *The Middle Kingdom.* (New York) 1848. p. 96.
5. Maclay, R.S. *Life Among The Chinese.* (New York) 1861. pp. 136-137.
6. *Albany Farmer's, Mechanic's and Workingman's Advocate.* April 10, 1830. n.p.
7. Hill, Herbert. "Anti-Oriental Agitation and the Rise of Working-Class Racism." *Society.* (10) January-February 1973. p. 52.
8. *Ibid.,* p.46.
9. *Ibid.,* p. 52.
10. Szasz, Thomas. *Ceremonial Chemistry.* (New York: Doubleday) 1974. Brecher, E.M. et al. *Licit and Illicit Drugs.* (Boston: Little Brown) 1972.
11. Miller, Stuart. *The Unwelcome Immigrant.* (Berkeley: U. of Cal Press). 1969. p. 9.
12. *Ibid.,* p. 162.
13. *Ibid.,* p. 162.
14. *Ibid.,* p. 163.
15. *Ibid.,* p. 164.
16. *Ibid.,* p. 163.
17. *Ibid.,* p. 163.
18. Terry, Charles and Mildred Pellens. *The Opium Problem.* (New York: Committee on Drug Addictions) 1928. p. 193.

19. Miller, Stuart. *The Unwelcome Immigrant*. (Berkeley: U. of Cal Press). 1969. p. 198.

20. *Ibid.*, pp. 163-164.

21. *New York Tribune*, October 20, 1905.

22. Miller, Stuart. *The Unwelcome Immigrant*. (Berkeley: U. of Cal Press). 1969. p. 185.

23. *Ibid.*, p. 184.

24. Kandall, Stephen. *Substance and Shadow*. (Harvard U.P.) 1996. p. 65.

25. Silver, Gary. *The Dope Chronicles: 1850-1950*. (New York: Harper and Row) 1974. p. 41.

26. Gilfoyle, Timothy. *City of Eros: New York City, Prostitution and the Commercialization of Sex 1790-1920*. (New York: Norton) 1992. p. 219.

27. Courtwright, David. *Dark Paradise*. (Harvard U.P.) 1982. p. 78.

28. Kane, H.H. *Opium-Smoking in America and China*. (New York: Putnams) 1882. p. 8.

29. *New York Times*, October 30, 1905. pt. 4, p.4.

30. Holden, Charles. "Chinese Slavery in America." *North American Review*. September 1897. p. 294.

31. Wright, Hamilton. "Report: International Opium." in *Opium Problem: Message*. p. 45.

32. Krivanek, Jara. *Heroin*. (Sydney: Allen and Unwin) 1988. p. 55.

33. Sante, Luc. *Lowlife*. (New York: Farrar, Straus) 1991. pp. 128-129.

34. *Leviticus 16:* 10, 20, 21.

35. Williams, George. *Wilderness and Paradise in Christian Thought*. (New York: Harper and Brothers) 1962. p. 13.

36. Szasz, Thomas. *Ceremonial Chemistry*. (New York: Doubleday) 1974. p. 111.

37. Metzger, Th. *Blood and Volts*. (New York: Autonomedia) 1996. pp. 117, 134, 163.
38. Girard, René. *Violence and the Sacred*. (Baltimore, MD: John Hopkins U.P.) 1977. p. 8.
39. Murray, Robert K. *Red Scare*. (Minneapolis: U of Minnesota Press) 1955.
40. Weir, William. *In The Shadow of the Dope Fiend*. (North Have, Connecticut: Archon) 1995. p. 40.
41. Murray, Robert K. *Red Scare*. (Minneapolis: U of Minnesota Press) 1955. p. 97.
42. Palmer, A. Mitchell. "Extent of the Bolshevik Infection Here." *Literary Digest*. LXIV. 1/17/1920. p. 13.
43. Herer, Jack. *Hemp and the Marijuana Conspiracy*. (Van Nuys, California: Hemp Publishing) 1985. p. 27.
44. Silver, Gary. *The Dope Chronicles: 1850-1950*. (New York: Harper and Row) 1974. pp. 120-121.
45. Black, Winifred. *Dope: the Story of the Living Dead*. (New York: Star Co.) 1928. pp. 15, 19, 23.
46. *Ibid.*, pp. 14, 77.
47. Herer, Jack. *Hemp and the Marijuana Conspiracy*. (Van Nuys, California: Hemp Publishing) 1985. p. 68.
48. Musto, David. *The American Disease*. (Yale U.P.) 1973. p. 212.
49. *Ibid.*, p. 195.
50. Weir, William. *In The Shadow of the Dope Fiend*. (North Haven, Connecticut: Archon) 1995. p. 45.
51. Hobson, Richmond P. "Heroin Heroes." *Saturday Evening Post*. September 20, 1924. p. 41.
52. Hobson, Richmond P. *Alcohol and the Human Race*. (New York: Fleming Revell Co.) 1919. pp. 33, 46, 90, 104, 109.

53. Hobson, Richmond P. Speech given to U.S. House of Representatives. December 22, 1914.
54. Hobson, Richmond P. *Alcohol and the Human Race.* (New York: Fleming Revell Co.) 1919. p. 182.
55. *Ibid.,* p. 107-109.
56. Furnas, Joseph. *The Life and Times of the Late Demon Rum.* (New York: Putnams) 1965. p. 316.
57. Weir, William. *In The Shadow of the Dope Fiend.* (North Haven, Connecticut: Archon) 1995. p. 24.
58. Furnas, Joseph. *The Life and Times of the Late Demon Rum.* (New York: Putnams) 1965. p. 317.
59. Sinclair, Andrew. *Prohibition: the Era of Excess.* (Boston: Little, Brown) 1962. p. 46.
60. *Ibid.,* p. 49.
61. Epstein, Edward. *Agency of Fear.* (New York: Putnams) 1977. p. 24.
62. Sheldon, Richard. *Richmond Pearson Hobson: the Military Hero as Reformer.* (Tucson: U. of Arizona thesis) 1970. p. 227.
63. Rumbarger, John. *Profits, Power and Prohibition.* (Albany, New York: SUNY Press) 1989. p. 177. Hobson, Richmond P. "Heroin Heroes." *Saturday Evening Post.* September 20, 1920. p. 42. and Speech given to U.S. House of Representatives. December 22, 1914.
64. Hobson, Richmond P. "Heroin Heroes." *Saturday Evening Post.* September 20, 1924. p. 41.
65. Hobson, Richmond P. Speech given to U.S. House of Representatives. December 22, 1914.
66. Hobson, Richmond P. "Heroin Heroes." *Saturday Evening Post.* September 20, 1924. p. 41.
67. Hobson, Richmond P. *Alcohol and the Human Race.* (New York: Fleming Revell Co.) 1919. p. 69.

68. *Ibid.,* p. 109.
69. *Time,* March 21, 1931. p. 52.
70. Weir, William. *In The Shadow of the Dope Fiend.* (North Haven, Connecticut: Archon) 1995. p. 43.
71. Hobson, Richmond P. "Heroin Heroes." *Saturday Evening Post.* September 20, 1924. p. 41.
72. Hobson, Richmond P. *Alcohol and the Human Race.* (New York: Fleming Revell Co.) 1919. p191.
73. Hobson, Richmond P. "One Million Americans Victim of Drug Habit." *New York Times.* November 9, 1924. Part 9, p.4.
74. Hobson, Richmond P. "Heroin Heroes." *Saturday Evening Post.* September 20, 1924. p. 42. Graham-Mulhall, Sara. *Opium: the Demon Flower.* 1926. pp. 60-61. Weir, William. *In The Shadow of the Dope Fiend.* (North Haven, Connecticut: Archon) 1995. p. 43.
75. Kandall, Stephen. *Substance and Shadow.* (Harvard U.P.) 1996. p. 106. Hobson, Richmond P. "Heroin Heroes." *Saturday Evening Post.* September 20, 1924. p. 42.
76. Hobson, Richmond P. "Heroin Heroes." *Saturday Evening Post.* September 20, 1924. p. 41. Musto, David, *The American Disease.* (Yale U.P.) 1973. p. 322.
77. Musto, David, *The American Disease.* (Yale U.P.) 1973. p. 326.
78. "Special Committee on Investigation Appointed March 25, 1918 by the Secretary of the Treasury: Traffic in Narcotics Drugs. (GPO) 1919. pp. 19-22.
79. Lambert, Alexander. "The Underlying Causes of the Narcotic Habit." *Modern Medicine.* (2) 1920. p. 8. Kandall, Stephen. *Substance and Shadow.* (Harvard

U.P.) 1996. p. 78. Wallis, Frederic. "The Menace of the Drug Addict." *Current History.* (21) 1925. p. 743.

80. Musto, David, *The American Disease.* (Yale U.P.) 1973. p. 254.
81. "History of Heroin." *Bulletin of Narcotics.* (5) 4-6, 1953. p. 7.
82. Musto, David. "Early History of Heroin in the U.S." in: *Addiction.* ed. Peter Bourne. (New York: Academic Press) 1974. p. 178.
83. Musto, David, *The American Disease.* (Yale U.P.) 1973. p. 121.
84. *Ibid.,* p. 102.
85. Kandall, Stephen. *Substance and Shadow.* (Harvard U.P.) 1996. p. 77.
86. Wallis, Frederic. "The Menace of the Drug Addict." *Current History.* (21) 1925. p. 740, 741, 743.
87. Trebach, Arnold. *The Heroin Solution.* (Yale U.P.) 1982. p. 48.
88. Musto, David. "Early History of Heroin in the U.S." in: *Addiction.* ed. Peter Bourne. (New York: Academic Press) 1974. p. 182.
89. Musto, David, *The American Disease.* (Yale U.P.) 1973. p. 201.
90. Szazs, Thomas. *Ceremonial Chemistry.* (New York: Doubleday). 1974. p. 4.
91. Musto, David, *The American Disease.* (Yale U.P.) 1973. p. 244.
92. Terry, Charles, and Mildred Pellens. *The Opium Problem.* (New York: Committee on Drug Addictions) 1928. p. 95.
93. Hobson, Richmond P. "One Million Americans Victim of Drug Habit." *New York Times.* November 9, 1924. Part 9, p.4.

94. "Death Among the Poppies." *New York American.* March 22, 1925. Editorial page.
95. Levin, David. ed. *What Happened in Salem?* (New York: Harcourt Brace) 1960. p. 97.
96. Mather, Cotton. *Wonders of The Invisible World.*
97. Terry, Charles, and Mildred Pellens. *The Opium Problem.* (New York: Committee on Drug Addictions) 1928. p. 122.
98. Levin, David. ed. *What Happened in Salem?* (New York: Harcourt Brace) 1960. p. 97.
99. *Ibid.,* p. 97.

Chapter Six
The New Orthodoxy

1.

Between 1880 and 1930, the image of the opiate user was transformed. In this 50-year transition period, competing medical ideologies fought to define "addiction." Inebriety, disease and psychopathy were the three main theories locked in struggle. At the end of this period, there was near-unanimity among doctors. Capping the triumph of the psychopathy theory, "drug addiction" was accepted in 1934 as a form of mental illness.

The theory of inebriety had steadily gained adherents as the 19th century waned. The American Association for the Cure of Inebriety was established in 1870 and its *Quarterly Journal of Inebriety* promoted the new explanation for the abuse of drugs. In England, Dr. Norman Kerr founded the Society for the Study of Inebriety in 1884. A more generalized malady than mere opiate use, inebriety was thought to be a medical condition. Still, it carried much of the moral opprobrium of the older, discarded "vice" model of opiate use. Kerr, while arguing that inebriety was a "mentally defective state which had its source in localized brain lesions," also wrote of moral decay and "moral perversions."[1] He acknowledged that organic causes of inebriety were seldom obvious, yet he was convinced of the existence of the "diathesis" in inebriates: a vague physical predisposition to use "narcotizing agents." In the U.S., doctors referred to "opium inebriates" and "morphine drunkards," whose brains contained a pathological mechanism which was triggered by repeated opiate intoxication.[2]

The theory of inebriety was built on two earlier psychological concepts: degeneration and neurasthenia. A first cousin, if not close sibling, to the eugenic theories prevalent at the same time, degeneration was a "morbid deviation from the normal human type, transmissible by heredity and subject to progressive deterioration across generations."[3] Though "vicious" environmental factors such as alcohol and opiate use might cause the initial degeneration, this theory held that there was a hereditary tendency in deviants. Thus the dependence on opiates was explained in the same way that certain ordinary conditions were explained: "your father had blue eyes; you'll have them too." "Your mother was an inebriate; you'll likely become one also."

If degeneration was the warp of the inebriety concept, then neurasthenia was the woof; woven together, they dominated medical thinking about opiates in the period 1880-1915. Meaning literally a weakness of the nerves, neurasthenia was a vaguely defined condition that could manifest in anything from an exhausted nervous system to excessive worry, headaches, sensitiveness, poor digestion, and the fatigue associated with Americans' hectic lives. Noting the strain and anxiety in the lives of the intellectual and economic elite, doctors who espoused the neurasthenia theory claimed that white middle- and upper-class people who used opiates to relieve their stresses often suffered resultant permanent damage to their nervous systems. A hereditary tendency to use inebriating substances coupled with the tensions and frantic pace of industrial urban life were thus blamed for the plague of "addiction." Given that in the 19th century the majority of opiate users were of the privileged classes, it made perfect sense to associate "addiction" with increasing demands placed on so-called brainworkers. Physicians had the highest incidence of morphine dependence. According to the neurasthenia theory, these doctors had a more sophisticated "nervous organization." Thus, they were more likely to be affected by drugs than blacks, recent European immigrants and other less exalted groups.

But the triumph of the forces of purity weakened this theory considerably. By the time the Harrison Act was implemented, the inebriety concept was discredited. This left two groups of "addiction experts" to fight it out for supremacy. The first consisted of those physicians who believed opiate users to be fundamentally ordinary people who developed their habits through no fault of their own. The second group argued that "addiction" was a symptom of psychopathy. In the two decades after the Harrison Act's passage, one theory was almost totally abandoned and the other was enshrined as the new orthodoxy.

The work of Jansen Mattison and Austin Pressey laid the foundation for Charles Terry, who campaigned vigorously for a change in therapeutic attitude toward drug users. Pressey summed up the position in six words: "Persons only get morphinism from morphine."[4] There was no diathesis, no neurasthenic condition, no degradation. Opiate dependence was caused by opiates. No blame was ascribed; no moral anathema was laid on the user. Opiates did have a powerful physiological effect, but no one was organically predisposed to become an "addict."

Continuing along these lines, Terry argued that the psychological state of the "drug addict" was entirely normal and natural, "...no more morbid than the psychology which prompts a thirsty man to drink, a hungry man to eat, a ravished woman to defend herself."[5] In other words, he blamed the drug, not the drug user. An "addict" was simply a person who'd contracted the disease of "addiction."

> The psychology of the drug addict is the psychology of the average human being. It is the psychology of you and me when in pain, of you and me when desiring relief, of you and me when either of us finds himself incapacitated and quite innocently in a situation he has been taught to believe is degrading. It is the psychology of self-defense, of self-protection, and it is the psychology arising from persecution, intolerance and ignorance.[6]

Other physicians — for a brief period — joined their voices to Terry's. Kennedy, in 1914, strove to separate medical and moral categories: "There is nothing inherent in the drug to cause his moral degradation." He too wrote of "sad victims" and "social pariahs." The next year, Alexander Lambert attempted to elicit sympathy for opiate users plagued by "haunting terrors" and "pitiful sufferings." In a survey of nearly 1,000 health officials in 1918, a special committee of investigation for the Secretary of the Treasury found that 542 still believed drug use to be a vice, while 425 considered it a disease. Talk of drug "victims" continued throughout the early 1920s.[7]

Willis Butler's concept of addiction was similar to Terry's. Director of the much-praised Shreveport maintenance clinic, Butler was convinced that the opiate habit was a continuing response to pain. Only with the elimination of their pain, did drug users stand a chance of breaking their habits. Butler had no tolerance for abstruse theorizing. He saw hundreds of men and women, rich and poor, who used opiates for relief of pain. "No matter what different persons may call the condition, the patient is a sick person, and as such is entitled to and should have proper consideration, care and treatment."[8]

Unlike Butler, Ernest S. Bishop was intensely interested in the exact mechanism of the "addiction disease." His anti-toxin theory was embraced by many in the 1910s as sufficient proof that the condition truly was a disease. He believed that the body produced anti-toxins in response to the presence of morphine. Supposedly, this explained a morphine-user's tolerance to the drug: the anti-toxins protected the user from what would be a lethal dose for a non-user. In the absence of fresh morphine, however, the anti-toxins decayed by an unknown process into toxins, causing the agonies of withdrawal. George Petty constructed a similar theory — claiming that "addicts" had no "structural lesion" on their brain, nor were they morally decayed. Opiates caused a self-generating toxemia, which in turn produced severe irritation of the nervous system: withdrawal.[9]

This theory, though it had some passionate adherents, did not have long to live. In 1921, the A.M.A.'s Committee on Narcotic Drugs bluntly condemned the "shallow pretense that drug addiction is a disease."[10] And physiological studies — finding no evidence of any anti-toxins produced by opiates — drummed the death march for Bishop's theory. The conflict between the various sides of the debate was so fierce that the downfall of the anti-toxin theory was touted by many as absolute disproof of the entire disease concept of addiction. Without concrete, physical proof, habituation and withdrawal were deemed utterly devoid of medical basis. When the dust and smoke of the conflict had cleared, there was only one theory left standing.

The Jaws of Death

2.

Temporarily triumphant, psychology in the 1920s was heralded as the most scientific, most up-to-date method for explaining and treating "drug addiction." Psychiatry was held at the time in far higher regard than now. Though it would be an exaggeration to say that a sense of optimism pervaded the field, still, much hope was placed on psychiatry: a new science, a young giant striding out to do battle with society's ills. Applying the psychiatric model to "addiction" promised great results, and was thought to be the next step in scientific progress.

The term "psychopath" now implies perversion, impulsive criminality, an absence of shame and remorse. It has been largely abandoned by psychological science, and is now a popular term more likely applied to Hitler, Charles Manson or nameless terrorists than a psychiatric patient. However, as the American notion of "addiction" crystallized in the 1920s, this word was the cornerstone of psychological theories regarding opiate use.

Merging the German concept of *psychopathische Persönlichkeit* with the British idea of moral insanity, psychiatrists in the 1920s developed a new explanation for unacceptable behaviors. Though not insane in the standard sense, psychopaths were thought to be controlled by a severe defect of character. They were inadequate human beings, perversely unaffected by moral standards, lacking self-control, common sense, truthfulness, and any social feeling. Searching for a better explanation of non-medical opiate habituation, psychiatrists found the term *psychopath* very useful.

The vagueness built into the theory of psychopathy is obvious to us now. Perhaps worse, there was a heavy dose of moralizing implicit in the concept. Though touted as a purely scientific theory, it was laden with the cultural assumptions out of which it sprang. Disciples of this new creed tried vigorously to separate themselves from Dope Fiend propagandists such as Richmond P. Hobson; still their efforts bear a striking similarity. Utter disregard for ethical thought, hopeless perversion, indecency, danger to society: these were the characteristics of psychopathy. But they might as well have come from the febrile alarms of Hobson and Harry Anslinger. A 1920 report published in *JAMA*, exhorting therapists to apply psychoanalysis to the "narcotic drug situation," claimed that treatment should teach the "drug addict to irradiate and sublimate this libido which is so wantonly wasting on the fetish of drug addiction." In the absence of therapy, society might awake to the fact that the opiate user "is an I.W.W., a bolshevik or what not."[11] Recognized now as a nearly useless term, psychopathy was used broadly within the therapeutic professions and rapidly entered common speech.

Trained as a psychiatrist, Lawrence Kolb was the person most responsible for establishing "addiction" as psychopathy. Though others asserted this view first, Kolb did more to popularize the belief than anyone, and created for this profession a five-tier psychopathic classification system: 1) iatrogenic "addicts," 2) innately pleasure-seeking individuals 3) those afflicted by "crystallized neuroses" 4) habitual criminals, and 5) inebriates. Kolb was convinced, and successfully convinced others, that the second and fourth categories in his system made up the majority of "addicts." For Kolb, pleasure was the crux of the problem. In four out of five of his categories, the opiate user had an exaggerated, unhealthy response to drug-induced pleasure. With a perverted moral sense, the psychopath had no qualms about indulging in self-destructive behaviors, especially if they gave temporary pleasure. In effect, this is an inversion of the "no pain, no gain" dogma. The more psychopathic a person was, the greater euphoria provided by opiates. In fact, Kolb claimed that only a psychopath can feel pleasure from a morphine or heroin injection. "Opiates apparently do not produce mental pleasure in stable persons," Kolb stated.[12] This equation of pleasure with mental illness or degeneracy; the repeated use of terms such as "perverse," "hopeless," "shameless," etc.; the insistence that there was a fundamental difference between normal people and "addicts;" all of these harmonize well with the more overtly moralistic Dope Fiend belief system. It may not be pushing the point too far to say that this is merely Puritan fear (of the physical realm, of the human body, of pleasure) tricked out in pseudo-scientific language.

Within the medical profession, Kolb's theories gained near-total hegemony by 1930. He was the most-cited expert in the field; even Charles Terry, whose ideas were antithetical to Kolb's, cites numerous articles which echo the psychopathic theory.[13] By the end of the 1920s, the battle was over and Kolb — along with his legion of followers — had won. In the literature of "addiction," Kolb's views had achieved the status of irrefutable dogma. The equation, "addict = psychopath," was established as official medical fact.

In 1934, the American Psychiatric Association put its stamp of approval on the notion. Its *New Standard Classi-*

fied Nomenclature of Disease lists "drug addiction" for the first time.[14]

Though labeling opiate use as a personality disorder has had far-reaching and unfortunate results, Kolb was truly sympathetic to his patients. For him, opiate use remained a medical problem, not primarily the concern of legal and religious authorities. Working for the U.S. Public Health Service and then as director of the Federal Narcotics "farm" at Lexington, Kentucky, he strove to create an environment that was humane and therapeutic. At Lexington, Kolb made what changes he could to provide treatment rather than punishment. As late as 1962 he complained that the U.S. suffered more from "misguided frenzy" to suppress "addiction" than from the so-called disease itself.[15]

However vigorously he fought against the ideas of Dope Fiend propagandists, still Kolb's efforts contributed to the demonization of the opiate user. The two dominant models — psychopathy and racial/genetic menace — in fact merged in the popular imagination. Since 1934, the Dope Fiend has been both sick and responsible for his sickness. He is mentally ill, morally corrupt, and contiguously dangerous. Combining one part religious condemnation with one part scientific diagnosis, we have the "addict" in his final form: a monster who should and can be controlled by the state. It matters very little now whether the police or government-financed mental health professionals do the actual controlling.

3.

When opiate use was enshrined in the canon of mental illnesses, its status as crime was not revoked, but deepened. The Harrison Act of 1914 made opiate users criminals; later Supreme Court rulings tightened the law's grasp. After 1934, the transgressive essence of opiates was more broadly defined as an affront to both civil law and natural law. According to the new orthodoxy, it became a menace to the well-being of American society and to the well-being of individual Americans. The opiate user had two choices: become a dependent vassal of the state or become absolutely excluded from society. Slave or scapegoat.

Thomas Szasz argues that much of the mental health establishment is a "gigantic pseudo-medical ritual." The suppression of certain drugs, as well as a wide variety of deviant behaviors is fundamentally a "ceremonial function." Szasz sums up the process this way: "as medical values have replaced religious values, medical rituals have taken the place of religious rituals."[16] Early eugenicists spoke of their work in terms of "sin" and "faith." The overtly religious philosophy of Richmond Hobson certainly influenced the final medical form of "addiction." Likewise, any drug-abuse expert who speaks in terms of purity and pollution (whether he knows it or not), of contagion and taint, updates older religious beliefs.

After 1934, legal and medical authorities in the U.S. became inseparably fused. There remained differences of opinion, turf battles and conflicting terminology; a powerful man such as Harry Anslinger could continue to resist the medicalization of drug use. But the idea that "addiction" is a condition requiring external control — by the state — has never since weakened. Even if we only consider sources of funding, it's clear that the medical/mental health professions are far more closely linked to the state than ever before. It may come as some surprise to modern readers the degree of difficulty the federal government experienced in establishing its legal right to control opiates. The Harrison Act was nominally a tax measure because it would have been far harder in 1914 for Washington to legislate against drugs on other grounds. Eight decades later, there's seldom a whisper of dissent when the state takes an increasingly aggressive role in social control. The various "wars on drugs" we've seen lately would have been unthinkable 100 years before, not because the level of anti-dope hysteria was lower, but because citizens would not have stood for such encroachments from the federal government.

With occasional exceptions (prohibition, anti-abortion efforts), the power of overtly religious law has experienced a steady decline since the fall of the Puritan theocracy. However, nominally secular social control (legal and medical) has increased to a point far beyond that which religion attained and has also taken up functions lost by the ritual of organized religion. For instance, confession is now performed in the therapist's office or on talk shows; marriage is now largely a matter for lawyers and judges, not ministers or priests.

Szasz argues very convincingly that the diagnosis of mental illness, psychopathy, personality disorder, etc., are far better understood as tools of social control than as objective scientific analysis. He does a masterful job in *The Manufacture of Madness* of tracing the shift from overt to covert religious law, of the establishment of medicine — especially the mental health professions — as religious control taking new forms. Fully comprehending these arguments can be a disturbing and disorienting experience. A reader who remains attached to the orthodox belief system that has pervaded American culture for the last half century will be angered, annoyed or appalled. But coming to this idea without the prejudices, bigotry and myopia which are the Puritan's legacy and the politician's stock-in-trade, we can gain a much better understanding of why the so-called drug problem continues to plague the U.S.

Drugs — and in particular, opiates — are not a foreign substance. They are profoundly American. The "addict" is not a new threat to American sanctity, but merely our current version of the dark-skinned menace. He has haunted our imagination since the Puritans waded ashore through the frozen waters of Massachusetts Bay. Mental illness is the 20th century version of a very old notion. It could not have been united with the Dope Fiend image until psychiatry and psychoanalysis were accepted as legitimate sciences. But the equation of badness and madness, social deviance with insanity, reaches back to precolonial Europe. Overt religious law may have weakened since the days of the Puritan commonwealth, but the impulses that drive this form of social control still remain strong, stronger perhaps than ever. They were born from, and continue to feed on, the deeply American ideals of purity and pollution.

The Birth of Heroin and
The Demonization of The Dope Fiend
216

Notes:

1. Harding, Geoffrey. *Opiate Addiction, Morality and Medicine.* (New York: St. Martins) 1988. pp. 59 & 60.
2. Terry, Charles and Milded Pellen. *The Opium Problem.* (New York: Committee on Drug Addictions) 1928. p. 102.
3. Courtwright, David. *Dark Paradise.* (Harvard U.P.) 1982. p. 127
4. Sterne, Albert. "Have Drug Addictions a Pathological Basis?" *JAMA.* (44) 1905. p. 612.
5. Terry, Charles. "Some Recent Experiments in Narcotics Control." *American Journal of Public Health.* (11) 1921. p. 41.
6. *Ibid.,* p. 41.
7. Terry, Charles and Milded Pellen. *The Opium Problem.* (New York: Committee on Drug Addictions) 1928. pp. 147, 148, 154, 109, 112.
8. Courtwright, David. *Dark Paradise.* (Harvard U.P.) 1982. p. 131.
9. Terry, Charles and Milded Pellen. *The Opium Problem.* (New York: Committee on Drug Addictions) 1928. p. 145.
10. Kandall, Stephen. *Substance and Shadow.* (Harvard U.P.) 1996. p. 97.
11. "Report of the Committee on the Narcotics Situation." *JAMA.* (74) May 8, 1920. p. 1326.
12. Kolb, Lawrence. "Pleasure and Deterioration from Narcotic Addiction." *Mental Hygiene.* (9) p. 723.

13. Terry, Charles and Milded Pellen. *The Opium Problem*. (New York: Committee on Drug Addictions) 1928. pp. 125, 127, 143, 163.
14. Menninger, Karl. *The Vital Balance*. (New York: Viking) 1963. p. 474.
15. Kolb, Lawrence. *"Drug Addiction": a Medical Problem*. (Springfield, Illinois: Charles C. Thomas Co.) 1962. p. 169.
16. Szasz, Thomas. *Ceremonial Chemistry*. (New York: Doubleday) 1974. p. 29.

Chronology

1869-1906	150,000 ovaries removed via "Battey's Operation"
1870-1900	Golden Age of clitoral excision
1882	First temperance education law in U.S.
1882	Chinese Exclusion Act
1883	Word "eugenics" first used by Galton
1887-1926	Eugenics studies
1888	Jack the Ripper
1891	First electric chair
1898	Heroin introduced
1899	Aspirin introduced
1903	Cocaine removed from Coca Cola
1904	Eugenics Records Office opens
1906	First Pure Food and Drug Act
1907	Indiana Sterilization Act
1909	U.S. prohibits opium importation for smoking
1910	Mann Act
1912	Kallikak family study published
1914	Harrison Act
1915	Rebirth of the K.K.K.
1916	*Passing of the Great Race* published
1919-1920	Red Scare
1919	*Alcohol and the Human Race* published

1920	Nazi party founded
1920	Prohibition begins
1921	Cigarettes illegal in 14 states
1923	Hobson switches to anti-dope crusading, founds "International Narcotics Education League"
1923-1924	Hitler in prison
1924	Manufacture of heroin prohibited in the U.S.
1925	*Mein Kampf* published
1927	Carrie Buck case
1928	Hobson inaugurates "Narcotics Education Week"
1930	Federal Bureau of Narcotics founded
1933	Prohibition ends
1933	Hitler comes to power
1934	"Addiction" becomes official mental health category in U.S.
1934	Hayes Code instituted in Hollywood to clean up American films
1934	German sterilization laws go into effect

Modern-day Vietnamese heroin label bears a similarity
to an early Bayer's emblem (see Chapter One)

YOU WILL ALSO WANT TO READ:

YOU WILL ALSO WANT TO READ:

☐ **85186 OPIUM FOR THE MASSES: A Practical Guide to Growing Poppies and Making Opium,** *by Jim Hogshire.* Everything you want to know about the beloved poppy and its amazing properties, including: What does the opium high feel like?; The stunning similarities between opium and your body's natural endorphins; Morphine and its derivatives; How to grow opium poppies; Sources for fertile poppy seeds; How to harvest the opium from a crop of poppies; How to make poppy tea; Other ways of making and ingesting opium; And much more! Also includes rare photographs and detailed information that bring this magnificent plant to life. *1994, 5½ x 8½, 112 pp, illustrated, soft cover.* $14.95.

☐ **85182 PSYCHEDELIC SHAMANISM: The Cultivation, Preparation and Shamanic Use of Psychotropic Plants,** *by Jim DeKorne.* From the author of *The Hydroponic Hot House* comes the boldest exploration of psychedelic plants ever since Terence McKenna's *Food of the Gods.* DeKorne is a "psychonaut" exploring the "imaginal realms" through personal experimentation and scholarly research. He guides the reader through the history and lore of psychotropic plants, with advice on how to handle the eerie "Entities" one encounters in "hyperspace." Plants and combinations covered include: Belladonna Alkaloids; D-Lysergic Acid Amide; Mescaline; Ayahuasca; Smokable DMT from Plants; Psilocybin; and more. *1994, 8½ x 11, 164 pp, illustrated, index, soft cover.* $19.95.

Loompanics Unlimited
PO Box 1197
Port Townsend, WA 98368

BOH8

Please send me the books I have checked above. I have enclosed $_____ which includes $4.95 for shipping and handling of the first $20.00 ordered. Add an additional $1 shipping for each additional $20 ordered. Washington residents include 7.9% sales tax.

Name _____

Address _____

City/State/Zip _____

YOU WILL ALSO WANT TO READ:

YOU WILL ALSO WANT TO READ:

YOU WILL ALSO WANT TO READ:

☐ **70050 PIRATE RADIO OPERATIONS, *by Andrew Yoder and Earl T. Gray*.** Pirate radio is one of the Communication Age's most fascinating developments! Now, for those hobbyists who yearn to learn the ins and outs of clandestine radio broadcasting, there's a wealth of knowledge available in *Pirate Radio Operations!* For the first time, there's a hands-on manual that fully explains the intricacies of this burgeoning pastime. Yoder has devoted his energies to pirate radio for years, and now he shares his practical expertise with the world. Complete with numerous photographs and illustrations that provide workable designs and schematics for all pirate radio buffs, this is the finest how-to book ever published on this subject. *1997, 5½ x 8½, 376 pp, illustrated, soft cover.* **$19.95.**

☐ **70051 ACCESS TO THE AIRWAVES, *by Allan H. Weiner, as told to Anita McCormick*.** Allan H. Weiner has always believed that the airwaves are free and rightfully belong to the people. The hardships that Weiner endured to bring Radio New York International and other pirate stations into being are legendary. The FCC's illegal seizure of his radio ship the *M/V Sarah* in 1987 made headlines around the world. Over the years, the FCC has targeted Weiner and done everything in its power to destroy his life. In spite of this, Weiner has persevered, and continues to work towards a future when the airwaves are open to all who choose to use them, and the world becomes a better place because of the free transmission of knowledge. His story is both a heartwarming tale of an electronic genius at work and a chilling indictment of governmental disregard for personal liberties and free speech. *1997, 5½ x 8½, 264 pp, soft cover.* $17.95.

Loompanics Unlimited
PO Box 1197
Port Townsend, WA 98368

BOH8

Please send me the books I have checked above. I have enclosed $_____ which includes $4.95 for shipping and handling of the first $20.00 ordered. Add an additional $1 shipping for each additional $20 ordered. Washington residents include 7.9% sales tax.

Name_____

Address _____

City/State/Zip_____

VISA and MasterCard accepted. 1-800-380-2230 for credit card orders *only.*
8am to 4pm, PST, Monday through Friday.

YOU WILL ALSO WANT TO READ:

☐ **94146 LOOMPANICS' GREATEST HITS, Articles and Features from the Best Book Catalog in the World,** *Edited by Michael Hoy.* A collection of articles and essays, cartoons and rants, gleaned from the pages of the Loompanics Unlimited book catalog. For over a decade, the Loompanics Catalog has served as a kiosk for writers from the far left, the far right and the *far out* — including Robert Anton Wilson, Kurt Saxon, Robert Shea and many, many others. A compendium of counterculture thought, this provocative book contains more than 75 features in all. *1990, 8½ x 11, 300 pp, illustrated, soft cover.* $14.95.

☐ **94293 LOOMPANICS UNLIMITED CONQUERS THE UNIVERSE, Articles and Features from The Best Book Catalog in the World,** *Edited by Michael Hoy.* Loompanics Unlimited has expanded its domain throughout the galaxies with 44 articles, stories, and essays in a mind-boggling compilation that will have every entity in space screaming in delight! Some of the most gifted writers on Earth have contributed to this compendium of literary masterfulness. We have also enlisted the aid of some of the planet's finest illustrators. The force was definitely with this talented group of creative troopers. Hey... we couldn't have conquered the universe without them! *1998, 8½ x 11, 224 pp, illustrated, soft cover.* $13.95.

Order any of the titles on this and the preceding pages and receive our large 1998 Main Catalog, *The Best Book Catalog In the World* **Free.** Or send $5.00 to receive it separately. See the catalog ad at the end of the book.

YOU WILL ALSO WANT TO READ:

☐ **14177 COMMUNITY TECHNOLOGY,** *by Karl Hess with an Introduction by Carol Moore.* In the 1970s, the late Karl Hess participated in a five-year social experiment in Washington D.C.'s Adam-Morgan neighborhood. Hess and several thousand others labored to make their neighborhood as self-sufficient as possible, turning to such innovative techniques as raising fish in basements, growing crops on rooftops and in vacant lots, installing self-contained bacteriological toilets, and planning a methanol plant to convert garbage to fuel. There was a newsletter and weekly community meetings, giving Hess and others a taste of participatory government that changed their lives forever. *1995, 5½ x 8½, 120 pp, soft cover.* $9.95.

☐ **13063 SURVIVAL BARTERING,** *by Duncan Long.* People barter for different reasons — to avoid taxes, obtain a better lifestyle, or just for fun. This book foresees a time when barter is a necessity. Three forms of barter; Getting good deals; Stockpiling for future bartering; Protecting yourself from rip-offs; And much more. Learning how to barter could be the best insurance you can find. *1986, 5½ x 8½, 56 pp, soft cover.* $8.00.

☐ **10060 OUR VANISHING PRIVACY, And What You Can Do To Protect Yourself,** *by Robert Ellis Smith.* This shocking book reveals how much strangers know about your private life. Someone's collecting information about your health, your finances, your love life. And they don't have your best interests at heart. *Our Vanishing Privacy* reveals the secrets of the snoops — what they know and how they get their information — and tells you what you need to know to fight back. Smith, the publisher of *Privacy Journal,* is one of the most outspoken advocates of privacy in the world. *1993, 5½ x 8½, 136 pp, soft cover.* $12.95.

Loompanics Unlimited
PO Box 1197
Port Townsend, WA 98368

BOH8

Please send me the books I have checked above. I have enclosed $_____ which includes $4.95 for shipping and handling of the first $20.00 ordered. Add an additional $1 shipping for each additional $20 ordered. Washington residents include 7.9% sales tax.

Name_____

Address _____

City/State/Zip_____

VISA and MasterCard accepted. 1-800-380-2230 for credit card orders *only.*
8am to 4pm, PST, Monday through Friday.

YOU WILL ALSO WANT TO READ:

Loompanics Unlimited
PO Box 1197
Port Townsend, WA 98368

BOH8

Please send me the books I have checked above. I have enclosed $_____ which includes $4.95 for shipping and handling of the first $20.00 ordered. Add an additional $1 shipping for each additional $20 ordered. Washington residents include 7.9% sales tax.

Name_____

Address _____

City/State/Zip_____

VISA and MasterCard accepted. 1-800-380-2230 for credit card orders *only.*
8am to 4pm, PST, Monday through Friday.

YOU WILL ALSO WANT TO READ:

YOU WILL ALSO WANT TO READ:

YOU WILL ALSO WANT TO READ:

☐ **91085 SECRETS OF A SUPER HACKER,** *by The Knightmare.* The most amazing book on computer hacking ever written! Step-by-step, illustrated details on the techniques used by hackers to get at your data including: ♦ Guessing Passwords ♦ Stealing Passwords ♦ Password Lists ♦ Social Engineering ♦ Reverse Social Engineering ♦ Crashing Electronic Bulletin Boards ♦ Dummy Screens ♦ Fake E-mail ♦ Trojan Horses ♦ Viruses ♦ Worms ♦ Trap Doors ♦ How To Keep From Getting Caught ♦ And Much More! The how-to text is highlighted with bare-knuckle tales of the Knightmare's hacks. No person concerned with computer security should miss this amazing manual of mayhem. *1994, 8½ x 11, 205 pp, illustrated, soft cover.* **$19.95.**

☐ **61152 DOCUMENT FRAUD AND OTHER CRIMES OF DECEPTION,** *by Jesse M. Greenwald.* Written by a 20-year practitioner of document fraud with 22 felonies and five prison terms to his credit, this book clearly explains: Computer equipment the forger needs, and alternative methods of acquiring it ♦ Necessary software ♦ How the forger gets the right paper ♦ The notary stamp ♦ How the forger fabricates checks, stock certificates, trust and quitclaim deeds, vehicle titles, and bonded credit cards ♦ Methods the forger employs to obtain alternative identification ♦ Insurance fraud ♦ How the forger makes his own credit cards ♦ How the forger sets up a phony but convincing office as a front ♦ Tenant and real estate scams the forger engages in ♦ and much, much more! The most informative book ever written on this subject! *1997, 5½ x 8½, 152 pp, illustrated, soft cover.* **$15.00.**

Order any of the above mentioned books and receive our large 1998 Main Catalog Free. Or send $5.00 to receive it separately. See our catalog ad on the next page.
